Service Application
Complete Self-Assessment Guide

The guidance in this Self-Assessment is based ⌐⌐ ⌐⌐⌐⌐⌐⌐ Application best practices and standards in business process architecture, design and quality management. The guidance is also based on the professional judgment of the individual collaborators listed in the Acknowledgments.

Notice of rights

Table of Contents

About The Art of Service

The Art of Service, Business Process Architects since 2000, is dedicated to helping stakeholders achieve excellence.

Defining, designing, creating, and implementing a process to solve a stakeholders challenge or meet an objective is the most valuable role... In EVERY group, company, organization and department.

Unless you're talking a one-time, single-use project, there should be a process. Whether that process is managed and implemented by humans, AI, or a combination of the two, it needs to be designed by someone with a complex enough perspective to ask the right questions.

Someone capable of asking the right questions and step back and say, 'What are we really trying to accomplish here? And is there a different way to look at it?'

With The Art of Service's Standard Requirements Self-Assessments, we empower people who can do just that — whether their title is marketer, entrepreneur, manager, salesperson, consultant, Business Process Manager, executive assistant, IT Manager, CIO etc... —they are the people who rule the future. They are people who watch the process as it happens, and ask the right questions to make the process work better.

Contact us when you need any support with this Self-Assessment and any help with templates, blue-prints and examples of standard documents you might need:

http://theartofservice.com
service@theartofservice.com

Acknowledgments

This checklist was developed under the auspices of The Art of Service, chaired by Gerardus Blokdyk.

Representatives from several client companies participated in the preparation of this Self-Assessment.

In addition, we are thankful for the design and printing services provided.

Included Resources - how to access

Included with your purchase of the book is the Service Application Self-Assessment Spreadsheet Dashboard which contains all questions and Self-Assessment areas and auto-generates insights, graphs, and project RACI planning - all with examples to get you started right away.

How? Simply send an email to
access@theartofservice.com
with this books' title in the subject to get the Service Application Self Assessment Tool right away.

You will receive the following contents with New and Updated specific criteria:

- The latest quick edition of the book in PDF

- The latest complete edition of the book in PDF, which criteria correspond to the criteria in...

- The Self-Assessment Excel Dashboard, and...

- Example pre-filled Self-Assessment Excel Dashboard to get familiar with results generation

- In-depth specific Checklists covering the topic

- Project management checklists and templates to assist with implementation

INCLUDES LIFETIME SELF ASSESSMENT UPDATES

Every self assessment comes with Lifetime Updates and Lifetime Free Updated Books. Lifetime Updates is an industry-first feature which allows you to receive verified self assessment updates, ensuring you always have the most accurate information at your fingertips.

Get it now- you will be glad you did - do it now, before you forget.

Send an email to **access@theartofservice.com** with this books' title in the subject to get the Service Application Self Assessment Tool right away.

Your feedback is invaluable to us

If you recently bought this book, we would love to hear from you! You can do this by writing a review on amazon (or the online store where you purchased this book) about your last purchase! As part of our continual service improvement process, we love to hear real client experiences and feedback.

How does it work?

To post a review on Amazon, just log in to your account and click on the Create Your Own Review button (under Customer Reviews) of the relevant product page. You can find examples of product reviews in Amazon. If you purchased from another online store, simply follow their procedures.

What happens when I submit my review?

Once you have submitted your review, send us an email at review@theartofservice.com with the link to your review so we can properly thank you for your feedback.

Purpose of this Self-Assessment

This Self-Assessment has been developed to improve understanding of the requirements and elements of Service Application, based on best practices and standards in business process architecture, design and quality management.

It is designed to allow for a rapid Self-Assessment to determine how closely existing management practices and procedures correspond to the elements of the Self-Assessment.

The criteria of requirements and elements of Service Application have been rephrased in the format of a Self-Assessment questionnaire, with a seven-criterion scoring system, as explained in this document.

In this format, even with limited background knowledge of

Service Application, a manager can quickly review existing operations to determine how they measure up to the standards. This in turn can serve as the starting point of a 'gap analysis' to identify management tools or system elements that might usefully be implemented in the organization to help improve overall performance.

How to use the Self-Assessment

On the following pages are a series of questions to identify to what extent your Service Application initiative is complete in comparison to the requirements set in standards.

To facilitate answering the questions, there is a space in front of each question to enter a score on a scale of '1' to '5'.

1 Strongly Disagree

2 Disagree

3 Neutral

4 Agree

5 Strongly Agree

Read the question and rate it with the following in front of mind:

'In my belief,
the answer to this question is clearly defined'.

There are two ways in which you can choose to interpret this statement;
1. how aware are you that the answer to the question is clearly defined
2. for more in-depth analysis you can choose to gather

evidence and confirm the answer to the question. This obviously will take more time, most Self-Assessment users opt for the first way to interpret the question and dig deeper later on based on the outcome of the overall Self-Assessment.

A score of '1' would mean that the answer is not clear at all, where a '5' would mean the answer is crystal clear and defined. Leave emtpy when the question is not applicable or you don't want to answer it, you can skip it without affecting your score. Write your score in the space provided.

After you have responded to all the appropriate statements in each section, compute your average score for that section, using the formula provided, and round to the nearest tenth. Then transfer to the corresponding spoke in the Service Application Scorecard on the second next page of the Self-Assessment.

Your completed Service Application Scorecard will give you a clear presentation of which Service Application areas need attention.

Service Application Scorecard Example

Example of how the finalized Scorecard can look like:

Service Application Scorecard

Your Scores:

BEGINNING OF THE SELF-ASSESSMENT:

CRITERION #1: RECOGNIZE

INTENT: Be aware of the need for change. Recognize that there is an unfavorable variation, problem or symptom.

In my belief, the answer to this question is clearly defined:

5 Strongly Agree

4 Agree

3 Neutral

2 Disagree

1 Strongly Disagree

1. What is the problem or issue?
<--- Score

2. Will new equipment/products be required to facilitate Service Application delivery, for example is new software needed?
<--- Score

3. Will Service Application deliverables need to be

tested and, if so, by whom?
<--- Score

4. Who needs to know about Service Application?
<--- Score

5. What problems are you facing and how do you consider Service Application will circumvent those obstacles?
<--- Score

6. How do you identify subcontractor relationships?
<--- Score

7. Who needs budgets?
<--- Score

8. Are losses recognized in a timely manner?
<--- Score

9. Looking at each person individually – does every one have the qualities which are needed to work in this group?
<--- Score

10. What resources or support might you need?
<--- Score

11. Are there recognized Service Application problems?
<--- Score

12. How much are sponsors, customers, partners, stakeholders involved in Service Application? In other words, what are the risks, if Service Application does not deliver successfully?

<--- Score

13. Are there regulatory / compliance issues?
<--- Score

14. Do you need different information or graphics?
<--- Score

15. Have you identified your Service Application key performance indicators?
<--- Score

16. Who else hopes to benefit from it?
<--- Score

17. How are training requirements identified?
<--- Score

18. What is the extent or complexity of the Service Application problem?
<--- Score

19. Which information does the Service Application business case need to include?
<--- Score

20. What needs to be done?
<--- Score

21. Can management personnel recognize the monetary benefit of Service Application?
<--- Score

22. Are employees recognized or rewarded for performance that demonstrates the highest levels of integrity?

<--- Score

23. What extra resources will you need?
<--- Score

24. What are the expected benefits of Service Application to the stakeholder?
<--- Score

25. Which needs are not included or involved?
<--- Score

26. Will it solve real problems?
<--- Score

27. Why the need?
<--- Score

28. What information do users need?
<--- Score

29. Are problem definition and motivation clearly presented?
<--- Score

30. Does the problem have ethical dimensions?
<--- Score

31. How do you recognize an objection?
<--- Score

32. Is it needed?
<--- Score

33. As a sponsor, customer or management, how important is it to meet goals, objectives?

51. Does your organization need more Service Application education?
<--- Score

52. Did you miss any major Service Application issues?
<--- Score

53. Is the need for organizational change recognized?
<--- Score

54. What does Service Application success mean to the stakeholders?
<--- Score

55. Will a response program recognize when a crisis occurs and provide some level of response?
<--- Score

56. What are the timeframes required to resolve each of the issues/problems?
<--- Score

57. How do you take a forward-looking perspective in identifying Service Application research related to market response and models?
<--- Score

58. Are there any revenue recognition issues?
<--- Score

59. Are controls defined to recognize and contain problems?
<--- Score

60. Is it clear when you think of the day ahead of you what activities and tasks you need to complete?

<--- Score

61. Does Service Application create potential expectations in other areas that need to be recognized and considered?
<--- Score

62. What activities does the governance board need to consider?
<--- Score

63. Are you dealing with any of the same issues today as yesterday? What can you do about this?
<--- Score

64. Are there Service Application problems defined?
<--- Score

65. What are your needs in relation to Service Application skills, labor, equipment, and markets?
<--- Score

66. What is the problem and/or vulnerability?
<--- Score

67. What are the stakeholder objectives to be achieved with Service Application?
<--- Score

68. How are you going to measure success?
<--- Score

69. What do employees need in the short term?
<--- Score

70. For your Service Application project, identify and

describe the business environment, is there more than one layer to the business environment?
<--- Score

71. Is the quality assurance team identified?
<--- Score

72. Do you recognize Service Application achievements?
<--- Score

73. What are the clients issues and concerns?
<--- Score

74. What Service Application coordination do you need?
<--- Score

75. What Service Application capabilities do you need?
<--- Score

76. Who defines the rules in relation to any given issue?
<--- Score

77. What is the recognized need?
<--- Score

78. When a Service Application manager recognizes a problem, what options are available?
<--- Score

79. To what extent would your organization benefit from being recognized as a award recipient?
<--- Score

80. What needs to stay?
<--- Score

81. Think about the people you identified for
your Service Application project and the project
responsibilities you would assign to them, what kind
of training do you think they would need to perform
these responsibilities effectively?
<--- Score

82. What are the minority interests and what amount
of minority interests can be recognized?
<--- Score

83. Where do you need to exercise leadership?
<--- Score

84. Do you have/need 24-hour access to key
personnel?
<--- Score

85. How does it fit into your organizational needs and
tasks?
<--- Score

86. Are employees recognized for desired behaviors?
<--- Score

87. Do you need to avoid or amend any Service
Application activities?
<--- Score

88. Who needs what information?
<--- Score

89. Why is this needed?
<--- Score

90. Would you recognize a threat from the inside?
<--- Score

91. What is the Service Application problem definition? What do you need to resolve?
<--- Score

92. What training and capacity building actions are needed to implement proposed reforms?
<--- Score

93. What vendors make products that address the Service Application needs?
<--- Score

94. Do you know what you need to know about Service Application?
<--- Score

95. How do you assess your Service Application workforce capability and capacity needs, including skills, competencies, and staffing levels?
<--- Score

Add up total points for this section:
_ _ _ _ _ = Total points for this section

Divided by: _ _ _ _ _ _ (number of statements answered) = _ _ _ _ _ _
Average score for this section

Transfer your score to the Service Application Index at the beginning of

the Self-Assessment.

CRITERION #2: DEFINE:

INTENT: Formulate the stakeholder problem. Define the problem, needs and objectives.

In my belief, the answer to this question is clearly defined:

5 Strongly Agree

4 Agree

3 Neutral

2 Disagree

1 Strongly Disagree

1. Are the Service Application requirements testable?
<--- Score

2. Are roles and responsibilities formally defined?
<--- Score

3. Is scope creep really all bad news?
<--- Score

4. How do you gather Service Application requirements?
<--- Score

5. Has a Service Application requirement not been met?
<--- Score

6. What is the worst case scenario?
<--- Score

7. How do you hand over Service Application context?
<--- Score

8. How will the Service Application team and the group measure complete success of Service Application?
<--- Score

9. Are required metrics defined, what are they?
<--- Score

10. Have specific policy objectives been defined?
<--- Score

11. Is the Service Application scope manageable?
<--- Score

12. What sort of initial information to gather?
<--- Score

13. What constraints exist that might impact the team?
<--- Score

14. Is there regularly 100% attendance at the

team meetings? If not, have appointed substitutes attended to preserve cross-functionality and full representation?
<--- Score

15. What scope to assess?
<--- Score

16. When is/was the Service Application start date?
<--- Score

17. What baselines are required to be defined and managed?
<--- Score

18. What is in the scope and what is not in scope?
<--- Score

19. Has the Service Application work been fairly and/or equitably divided and delegated among team members who are qualified and capable to perform the work? Has everyone contributed?
<--- Score

20. Is there a critical path to deliver Service Application results?
<--- Score

21. Are audit criteria, scope, frequency and methods defined?
<--- Score

22. Has the direction changed at all during the course of Service Application? If so, when did it change and why?
<--- Score

23. How would you define the culture at your organization, how susceptible is it to Service Application changes?
<--- Score

24. What is a worst-case scenario for losses?
<--- Score

25. What are (control) requirements for Service Application Information?
<--- Score

26. Is Service Application required?
<--- Score

27. Where can you gather more information?
<--- Score

28. How is the team tracking and documenting its work?
<--- Score

29. Scope of sensitive information?
<--- Score

30. How do you manage changes in Service Application requirements?
<--- Score

31. What is the scope of the Service Application work?
<--- Score

32. If substitutes have been appointed, have they been briefed on the Service Application goals and received regular communications as to the progress

to date?
<--- Score

33. Is Service Application currently on schedule according to the plan?
<--- Score

34. Is the work to date meeting requirements?
<--- Score

35. Do you have organizational privacy requirements?
<--- Score

36. Has/have the customer(s) been identified?
<--- Score

37. What knowledge or experience is required?
<--- Score

38. Who are the Service Application improvement team members, including Management Leads and Coaches?
<--- Score

39. Is there a completed, verified, and validated high-level 'as is' (not 'should be' or 'could be') stakeholder process map?
<--- Score

40. When are meeting minutes sent out? Who is on the distribution list?
<--- Score

41. What are the core elements of the Service Application business case?
<--- Score

42. Is Service Application linked to key stakeholder goals and objectives?
<--- Score

43. How do you gather the stories?
<--- Score

44. What sources do you use to gather information for a Service Application study?
<--- Score

45. The political context: who holds power?
<--- Score

46. What is the definition of Service Application excellence?
<--- Score

47. Is there a Service Application management charter, including stakeholder case, problem and goal statements, scope, milestones, roles and responsibilities, communication plan?
<--- Score

48. Has everyone on the team, including the team leaders, been properly trained?
<--- Score

49. Will team members perform Service Application work when assigned and in a timely fashion?
<--- Score

50. Has a high-level 'as is' process map been completed, verified and validated?
<--- Score

51. What system do you use for gathering Service Application information?
<--- Score

52. Are customer(s) identified and segmented according to their different needs and requirements?
<--- Score

53. What Service Application requirements should be gathered?
<--- Score

54. How do you manage unclear Service Application requirements?
<--- Score

55. What critical content must be communicated – who, what, when, where, and how?
<--- Score

56. Is data collected and displayed to better understand customer(s) critical needs and requirements.
<--- Score

57. Are the Service Application requirements complete?
<--- Score

58. How do you think the partners involved in Service Application would have defined success?
<--- Score

59. What is the scope?
<--- Score

60. How are consistent Service Application definitions important?

<--- Score

61. How does the Service Application manager ensure against scope creep?

<--- Score

62. Why are you doing Service Application and what is the scope?

<--- Score

63. Has anyone else (internal or external to the group) attempted to solve this problem or a similar one before? If so, what knowledge can be leveraged from these previous efforts?

<--- Score

64. Have all basic functions of Service Application been defined?

<--- Score

65. How do you keep key subject matter experts in the loop?

<--- Score

66. In what way can you redefine the criteria of choice clients have in your category in your favor?

<--- Score

67. What would be the goal or target for a Service Application's improvement team?

<--- Score

68. Has your scope been defined?

<--- Score

69. How will variation in the actual durations of each activity be dealt with to ensure that the expected Service Application results are met?
<--- Score

70. What is in scope?
<--- Score

71. How do you gather requirements?
<--- Score

72. How did the Service Application manager receive input to the development of a Service Application improvement plan and the estimated completion dates/times of each activity?
<--- Score

73. Have the customer needs been translated into specific, measurable requirements? How?
<--- Score

74. What are the boundaries of the scope? What is in bounds and what is not? What is the start point? What is the stop point?
<--- Score

75. Is there a completed SIPOC representation, describing the Suppliers, Inputs, Process, Outputs, and Customers?
<--- Score

76. Are different versions of process maps needed to account for the different types of inputs?
<--- Score

77. What was the context?
<--- Score

78. What are the Service Application tasks and definitions?
<--- Score

79. What is out of scope?
<--- Score

80. Is the current 'as is' process being followed? If not, what are the discrepancies?
<--- Score

81. What are the requirements for audit information?
<--- Score

82. Do you all define Service Application in the same way?
<--- Score

83. What are the rough order estimates on cost savings/opportunities that Service Application brings?
<--- Score

84. Has the improvement team collected the 'voice of the customer' (obtained feedback – qualitative and quantitative)?
<--- Score

85. What specifically is the problem? Where does it occur? When does it occur? What is its extent?
<--- Score

86. How often are the team meetings?
<--- Score

87. What is the scope of the Service Application effort?
<--- Score

88. Do the problem and goal statements meet the SMART criteria (specific, measurable, attainable, relevant, and time-bound)?
<--- Score

89. Has a team charter been developed and communicated?
<--- Score

90. What gets examined?
<--- Score

91. How and when will the baselines be defined?
<--- Score

92. Are all requirements met?
<--- Score

93. Do you have a Service Application success story or case study ready to tell and share?
<--- Score

94. Will a Service Application production readiness review be required?
<--- Score

95. Is there any additional Service Application definition of success?
<--- Score

96. When is the estimated completion date?
<--- Score

97. What information do you gather?
<--- Score

98. What is out-of-scope initially?
<--- Score

99. Are approval levels defined for contracts and supplements to contracts?
<--- Score

100. Is the team equipped with available and reliable resources?
<--- Score

101. Is the Service Application scope complete and appropriately sized?
<--- Score

102. Are accountability and ownership for Service Application clearly defined?
<--- Score

103. Are there different segments of customers?
<--- Score

104. Have all of the relationships been defined properly?
<--- Score

105. What Service Application services do you require?
<--- Score

106. How was the 'as is' process map developed, reviewed, verified and validated?
<--- Score

107. What are the record-keeping requirements of Service Application activities?
<--- Score

108. Has a project plan, Gantt chart, or similar been developed/completed?
<--- Score

109. What defines best in class?
<--- Score

110. What are the compelling stakeholder reasons for embarking on Service Application?
<--- Score

111. What is the scope of Service Application?
<--- Score

112. Who approved the Service Application scope?
<--- Score

113. Who is gathering Service Application information?
<--- Score

114. What scope do you want your strategy to cover?
<--- Score

115. What key stakeholder process output measure(s) does Service Application leverage and how?
<--- Score

116. Who is gathering information?
<--- Score

117. Does the team have regular meetings?
<--- Score

118. How would you define Service Application leadership?
<--- Score

119. What is the definition of success?
<--- Score

120. What is the context?
<--- Score

121. What are the Roles and Responsibilities for each team member and its leadership? Where is this documented?
<--- Score

122. Is there a clear Service Application case definition?
<--- Score

123. Is the improvement team aware of the different versions of a process: what they think it is vs. what it actually is vs. what it should be vs. what it could be?
<--- Score

124. Are resources adequate for the scope?
<--- Score

125. Is it clearly defined in and to your organization what you do?
<--- Score

126. Are task requirements clearly defined?
<--- Score

127. What intelligence can you gather?
<--- Score

128. Is full participation by members in regularly held team meetings guaranteed?
<--- Score

129. Will team members regularly document their Service Application work?
<--- Score

130. How do you catch Service Application definition inconsistencies?
<--- Score

131. What information should you gather?
<--- Score

132. What are the tasks and definitions?
<--- Score

133. What customer feedback methods were used to solicit their input?
<--- Score

134. Who defines (or who defined) the rules and roles?
<--- Score

135. How do you build the right business case?
<--- Score

136. Is special Service Application user knowledge

required?
<--- Score

137. How can the value of Service Application be defined?
<--- Score

138. Are there any constraints known that bear on the ability to perform Service Application work? How is the team addressing them?
<--- Score

139. Is the team adequately staffed with the desired cross-functionality? If not, what additional resources are available to the team?
<--- Score

140. What are the dynamics of the communication plan?
<--- Score

Add up total points for this section:
_____ = Total points for this section

Divided by: _____ (number of
statements answered) = _____
Average score for this section

Transfer your score to the Service
Application Index at the beginning of
the Self-Assessment.

CRITERION #3: MEASURE:

INTENT: Gather the correct data.
Measure the current performance and
evolution of the situation.

In my belief, the answer to this
question is clearly defined:

5 Strongly Agree

4 Agree

3 Neutral

2 Disagree

1 Strongly Disagree

1. Do you aggressively reward and promote the
people who have the biggest impact on creating
excellent Service Application services/products?
<--- Score

2. What are the current costs of the Service
Application process?
<--- Score

3. How will you measure your Service Application effectiveness?
<--- Score

4. What are the costs and benefits?
<--- Score

5. How do your measurements capture actionable Service Application information for use in exceeding your customers expectations and securing your customers engagement?
<--- Score

6. What disadvantage does this cause for the user?
<--- Score

7. Which Service Application impacts are significant?
<--- Score

8. Are there any easy-to-implement alternatives to Service Application? Sometimes other solutions are available that do not require the cost implications of a full-blown project?
<--- Score

9. Is the cost worth the Service Application effort ?
<--- Score

10. What causes innovation to fail or succeed in your organization?
<--- Score

11. What are the estimated costs of proposed changes?
<--- Score

12. How do you quantify and qualify impacts?
<--- Score

13. Are indirect costs charged to the Service Application program?
<--- Score

14. Among the Service Application product and service cost to be estimated, which is considered hardest to estimate?
<--- Score

15. Did you tackle the cause or the symptom?
<--- Score

16. What can be used to verify compliance?
<--- Score

17. What happens if cost savings do not materialize?
<--- Score

18. Which measures and indicators matter?
<--- Score

19. What methods are feasible and acceptable to estimate the impact of reforms?
<--- Score

20. Are missed Service Application opportunities costing your organization money?
<--- Score

21. Who should receive measurement reports?
<--- Score

22. How to cause the change?

<--- Score

23. How do you verify and validate the Service Application data?
<--- Score

24. What details are required of the Service Application cost structure?
<--- Score

25. What does a Test Case verify?
<--- Score

26. What do you measure and why?
<--- Score

27. What relevant entities could be measured?
<--- Score

28. How do you verify your resources?
<--- Score

29. How do you verify performance?
<--- Score

30. How will effects be measured?
<--- Score

31. Does the Service Application task fit the client's priorities?
<--- Score

32. What do people want to verify?
<--- Score

33. Does management have the right priorities

among projects?
<--- Score

34. Have you made assumptions about the shape of the future, particularly its impact on your customers and competitors?
<--- Score

35. What causes investor action?
<--- Score

36. Are supply costs steady or fluctuating?
<--- Score

37. What is an unallowable cost?
<--- Score

38. What are the strategic priorities for this year?
<--- Score

39. What does losing customers cost your organization?
<--- Score

40. How do you measure success?
<--- Score

41. Are you aware of what could cause a problem?
<--- Score

42. How will costs be allocated?
<--- Score

43. What measurements are being captured?
<--- Score

44. What users will be impacted?
<--- Score

45. Do you have a flow diagram of what happens?
<--- Score

46. What are the types and number of measures to use?
<--- Score

47. Where is the cost?
<--- Score

48. What causes mismanagement?
<--- Score

49. What are you verifying?
<--- Score

50. What are the Service Application investment costs?
<--- Score

51. What could cause you to change course?
<--- Score

52. What is the Service Application business impact?
<--- Score

53. Why do the measurements/indicators matter?
<--- Score

54. How are measurements made?
<--- Score

55. How do you verify the Service Application

requirements quality?
<--- Score

56. Is the solution cost-effective?
<--- Score

57. Was a business case (cost/benefit) developed?
<--- Score

58. How frequently do you track Service Application measures?
<--- Score

59. How can you reduce the costs of obtaining inputs?
<--- Score

60. What are your operating costs?
<--- Score

61. Where can you go to verify the info?
<--- Score

62. Are the units of measure consistent?
<--- Score

63. How do you verify and develop ideas and innovations?
<--- Score

64. How sensitive must the Service Application strategy be to cost?
<--- Score

65. What is your decision requirements diagram?
<--- Score

66. What tests verify requirements?
<--- Score

67. Do you have any cost Service Application limitation requirements?
<--- Score

68. How can you measure the performance?
<--- Score

69. How do you aggregate measures across priorities?
<--- Score

70. What is the cause of any Service Application gaps?
<--- Score

71. What are your primary costs, revenues, assets?
<--- Score

72. How are costs allocated?
<--- Score

73. Do you effectively measure and reward individual and team performance?
<--- Score

74. What are the costs of delaying Service Application action?
<--- Score

75. How long to keep data and how to manage retention costs?
<--- Score

76. Are there competing Service Application priorities?

<--- Score

77. What is measured? Why?
<--- Score

78. What measurements are possible, practicable and meaningful?
<--- Score

79. Are the Service Application benefits worth its costs?
<--- Score

80. What evidence is there and what is measured?
<--- Score

81. How much does it cost?
<--- Score

82. How will success or failure be measured?
<--- Score

83. How will you measure success?
<--- Score

84. What are the costs?
<--- Score

85. What is the total cost related to deploying Service Application, including any consulting or professional services?
<--- Score

86. What is your Service Application quality cost segregation study?
<--- Score

87. Where is it measured?

<--- Score

88. How will measures be used to manage and adapt?

<--- Score

89. How can a Service Application test verify your ideas or assumptions?

<--- Score

90. Does a Service Application quantification method exist?

<--- Score

91. What are the uncertainties surrounding estimates of impact?

<--- Score

92. How is performance measured?

<--- Score

93. How do you measure variability?

<--- Score

94. When a disaster occurs, who gets priority?

<--- Score

95. Have design-to-cost goals been established?

<--- Score

96. What does your operating model cost?

<--- Score

97. Are Service Application vulnerabilities categorized and prioritized?

<--- Score

98. Will Service Application have an impact on current business continuity, disaster recovery processes and/or infrastructure?
<--- Score

99. What would be a real cause for concern?
<--- Score

100. How can you measure Service Application in a systematic way?
<--- Score

101. What would it cost to replace your technology?
<--- Score

102. Do you have an issue in getting priority?
<--- Score

103. What potential environmental factors impact the Service Application effort?
<--- Score

104. Are you able to realize any cost savings?
<--- Score

105. Do the benefits outweigh the costs?
<--- Score

106. Why do you expend time and effort to implement measurement, for whom?
<--- Score

107. Which costs should be taken into account?
<--- Score

108. How is the value delivered by Service Application being measured?
<--- Score

109. When are costs are incurred?
<--- Score

110. How will your organization measure success?
<--- Score

111. How can you manage cost down?
<--- Score

112. What harm might be caused?
<--- Score

113. What is the cost of rework?
<--- Score

114. How is progress measured?
<--- Score

115. What could cause delays in the schedule?
<--- Score

116. Has a cost center been established?
<--- Score

117. What is the root cause(s) of the problem?
<--- Score

118. How do you prevent mis-estimating cost?
<--- Score

119. What are the operational costs after Service

Application deployment?
<--- Score

120. How do you measure efficient delivery of Service Application services?
<--- Score

121. Have you included everything in your Service Application cost models?
<--- Score

122. What are hidden Service Application quality costs?
<--- Score

123. What are the costs of reform?
<--- Score

124. What is the total fixed cost?
<--- Score

125. Are the measurements objective?
<--- Score

126. When should you bother with diagrams?
<--- Score

127. How can you reduce costs?
<--- Score

128. What are your customers expectations and measures?
<--- Score

129. What drives O&M cost?
<--- Score

130. What are the Service Application key cost drivers?
<--- Score

131. How do you verify the authenticity of the data and information used?
<--- Score

132. Are you taking your company in the direction of better and revenue or cheaper and cost?
<--- Score

133. Who pays the cost?
<--- Score

134. How do you verify if Service Application is built right?
<--- Score

Add up total points for this section:
_ _ _ _ _ = Total points for this section

Divided by: _ _ _ _ _ _ (number of statements answered) = _ _ _ _ _ _
Average score for this section

Transfer your score to the Service Application Index at the beginning of the Self-Assessment.

CRITERION #4: ANALYZE:

INTENT: Analyze causes, assumptions and hypotheses.

In my belief, the answer to this question is clearly defined:

5 Strongly Agree

4 Agree

3 Neutral

2 Disagree

1 Strongly Disagree

1. Were there any improvement opportunities identified from the process analysis?
<--- Score

2. Do you understand your management processes today?
<--- Score

3. Is there an established change management process?

<--- Score

4. Have any additional benefits been identified that will result from closing all or most of the gaps?
<--- Score

5. What methods do you use to gather Service Application data?
<--- Score

6. Was a detailed process map created to amplify critical steps of the 'as is' stakeholder process?
<--- Score

7. When should a process be art not science?
<--- Score

8. How can risk management be tied procedurally to process elements?
<--- Score

9. Is the gap/opportunity displayed and communicated in financial terms?
<--- Score

10. What other organizational variables, such as reward systems or communication systems, affect the performance of this Service Application process?
<--- Score

11. What tools were used to generate the list of possible causes?
<--- Score

12. How much data can be collected in the given timeframe?

<--- Score

13. Do staff qualifications match your project?
<--- Score

14. How will corresponding data be collected?
<--- Score

15. What types of data do your Service Application indicators require?
<--- Score

16. What output to create?
<--- Score

17. What quality tools were used to get through the analyze phase?
<--- Score

18. Think about some of the processes you undertake within your organization, which do you own?
<--- Score

19. What is the Value Stream Mapping?
<--- Score

20. Do you, as a leader, bounce back quickly from setbacks?
<--- Score

21. What is the output?
<--- Score

22. What are your current levels and trends in key measures or indicators of Service Application product and process performance that are important to and

directly serve your customers? How do these results compare with the performance of your competitors and other organizations with similar offerings?
<--- Score

23. What is the Service Application Driver?
<--- Score

24. An organizationally feasible system request is one that considers the mission, goals and objectives of the organization, key questions are: is the Service Application solution request practical and will it solve a problem or take advantage of an opportunity to achieve company goals?
<--- Score

25. What do you need to qualify?
<--- Score

26. What are the Service Application business drivers?
<--- Score

27. What were the financial benefits resulting from any 'ground fruit or low-hanging fruit' (quick fixes)?
<--- Score

28. What are the revised rough estimates of the financial savings/opportunity for Service Application improvements?
<--- Score

29. What are your best practices for minimizing Service Application project risk, while demonstrating incremental value and quick wins throughout the Service Application project lifecycle?
<--- Score

30. Is the Service Application process severely broken such that a re-design is necessary?
<--- Score

31. What process improvements will be needed?
<--- Score

32. How do you ensure that the Service Application opportunity is realistic?
<--- Score

33. Are Service Application changes recognized early enough to be approved through the regular process?
<--- Score

34. What Service Application data will be collected?
<--- Score

35. Has an output goal been set?
<--- Score

36. Who qualifies to gain access to data?
<--- Score

37. Think about the functions involved in your Service Application project, what processes flow from these functions?
<--- Score

38. Do your contracts/agreements contain data security obligations?
<--- Score

39. What successful thing are you doing today that may be blinding you to new growth opportunities?

<--- Score

40. How do you identify specific Service Application investment opportunities and emerging trends?
<--- Score

41. What did the team gain from developing a sub-process map?
<--- Score

42. What are your outputs?
<--- Score

43. What are the best opportunities for value improvement?
<--- Score

44. Are your outputs consistent?
<--- Score

45. What are evaluation criteria for the output?
<--- Score

46. Are all staff in core Service Application subjects Highly Qualified?
<--- Score

47. What are the processes for audit reporting and management?
<--- Score

48. What are the personnel training and qualifications required?
<--- Score

49. What, related to, Service Application processes

does your organization outsource?
<--- Score

50. Are all team members qualified for all tasks?
<--- Score

51. Where is the data coming from to measure compliance?
<--- Score

52. How is the data gathered?
<--- Score

53. How do you use Service Application data and information to support organizational decision making and innovation?
<--- Score

54. How is the way you as the leader think and process information affecting your organizational culture?
<--- Score

55. How was the detailed process map generated, verified, and validated?
<--- Score

56. What Service Application data should be managed?
<--- Score

57. Is the final output clearly identified?
<--- Score

58. What is your organizations system for selecting qualified vendors?
<--- Score

59. How do mission and objectives affect the Service Application processes of your organization?
<--- Score

60. How many input/output points does it require?
<--- Score

61. Who will facilitate the team and process?
<--- Score

62. What are the disruptive Service Application technologies that enable your organization to radically change your business processes?
<--- Score

63. How is the Service Application Value Stream Mapping managed?
<--- Score

64. What Service Application data should be collected?
<--- Score

65. Do your leaders quickly bounce back from setbacks?
<--- Score

66. Do you have the authority to produce the output?
<--- Score

67. How often will data be collected for measures?
<--- Score

68. Have you defined which data is gathered how?
<--- Score

69. What internal processes need improvement?
<--- Score

70. Has data output been validated?
<--- Score

71. How is Service Application data gathered?
<--- Score

72. Is there any way to speed up the process?
<--- Score

73. Who is involved in the management review process?
<--- Score

74. How will the change process be managed?
<--- Score

75. Do quality systems drive continuous improvement?
<--- Score

76. What data is gathered?
<--- Score

77. What other jobs or tasks affect the performance of the steps in the Service Application process?
<--- Score

78. How does the organization define, manage, and improve its Service Application processes?
<--- Score

79. What qualifications and skills do you need?

<--- Score

80. What systems/processes must you excel at?
<--- Score

81. Is the suppliers process defined and controlled?
<--- Score

82. What are the Service Application design outputs?
<--- Score

83. Do your employees have the opportunity to do what they do best everyday?
<--- Score

84. How do you promote understanding that opportunity for improvement is not criticism of the status quo, or the people who created the status quo?
<--- Score

85. What were the crucial 'moments of truth' on the process map?
<--- Score

86. Record-keeping requirements flow from the records needed as inputs, outputs, controls and for transformation of a Service Application process, are the records needed as inputs to the Service Application process available?
<--- Score

87. How will the data be checked for quality?
<--- Score

88. What are your key performance measures or indicators and in-process measures for the control

and improvement of your Service Application processes?
<--- Score

89. What are your current levels and trends in key Service Application measures or indicators of product and process performance that are important to and directly serve your customers?
<--- Score

90. Should you invest in industry-recognized qualifications?
<--- Score

91. Is the performance gap determined?
<--- Score

92. How do you implement and manage your work processes to ensure that they meet design requirements?
<--- Score

93. What controls do you have in place to protect data?
<--- Score

94. How will the Service Application data be captured?
<--- Score

95. What are the necessary qualifications?
<--- Score

96. What Service Application metrics are outputs of the process?
<--- Score

97. What is the complexity of the output produced?
<--- Score

98. Were Pareto charts (or similar) used to portray the 'heavy hitters' (or key sources of variation)?
<--- Score

99. Identify an operational issue in your organization, for example, could a particular task be done more quickly or more efficiently by Service Application?
<--- Score

100. Who is involved with workflow mapping?
<--- Score

101. Is data and process analysis, root cause analysis and quantifying the gap/opportunity in place?
<--- Score

102. What qualifications do Service Application leaders need?
<--- Score

103. Have the problem and goal statements been updated to reflect the additional knowledge gained from the analyze phase?
<--- Score

104. What will drive Service Application change?
<--- Score

105. What is the oversight process?
<--- Score

106. Is the required Service Application data

gathered?
<--- Score

107. How do your work systems and key work processes relate to and capitalize on your core competencies?
<--- Score

108. What does the data say about the performance of the stakeholder process?
<--- Score

109. Is there a strict change management process?
<--- Score

110. Who gets your output?
<--- Score

111. Can you add value to the current Service Application decision-making process (largely qualitative) by incorporating uncertainty modeling (more quantitative)?
<--- Score

112. What qualifies as competition?
<--- Score

113. What is the cost of poor quality as supported by the team's analysis?
<--- Score

114. What kind of crime could a potential new hire have committed that would not only not disqualify him/her from being hired by your organization, but would actually indicate that he/she might be a particularly good fit?

<--- Score

115. Was a cause-and-effect diagram used to explore the different types of causes (or sources of variation)?
<--- Score

116. What conclusions were drawn from the team's data collection and analysis? How did the team reach these conclusions?
<--- Score

117. What are your Service Application processes?
<--- Score

118. What resources go in to get the desired output?
<--- Score

119. What is your organizations process which leads to recognition of value generation?
<--- Score

120. How are outputs preserved and protected?
<--- Score

121. How difficult is it to qualify what Service Application ROI is?
<--- Score

122. How is data used for program management and improvement?
<--- Score

123. What qualifications are necessary?
<--- Score

124. What qualifications are needed?

<--- Score

125. What Service Application data do you gather or use now?
<--- Score

126. Where is Service Application data gathered?
<--- Score

127. How do you measure the operational performance of your key work systems and processes, including productivity, cycle time, and other appropriate measures of process effectiveness, efficiency, and innovation?
<--- Score

128. Are you missing Service Application opportunities?
<--- Score

129. What training and qualifications will you need?
<--- Score

130. What tools were used to narrow the list of possible causes?
<--- Score

131. What information qualified as important?
<--- Score

132. How do you define collaboration and team output?
<--- Score

133. Who owns what data?
<--- Score

134. Were any designed experiments used to generate additional insight into the data analysis?
<--- Score

135. What process should you select for improvement?
<--- Score

Add up total points for this section:
_ _ _ _ _ = Total points for this section

Divided by: _ _ _ _ _ _ (number of statements answered) = _ _ _ _ _ _
Average score for this section

Transfer your score to the Service Application Index at the beginning of the Self-Assessment.

CRITERION #5: IMPROVE:

INTENT: Develop a practical solution. Innovate, establish and test the solution and to measure the results.

In my belief, the answer to this question is clearly defined:

5 Strongly Agree

4 Agree

3 Neutral

2 Disagree

1 Strongly Disagree

1. What should a proof of concept or pilot accomplish?
<--- Score

2. What is the team's contingency plan for potential problems occurring in implementation?
<--- Score

3. How will you recognize and celebrate results?

<--- Score

4. What are the expected Service Application results?
<--- Score

5. What is the Service Application's sustainability risk?
<--- Score

6. How do you measure risk?
<--- Score

7. Is the Service Application solution sustainable?
<--- Score

8. Is there a high likelihood that any recommendations will achieve their intended results?
<--- Score

9. What alternative responses are available to manage risk?
<--- Score

10. How do you mitigate Service Application risk?
<--- Score

11. Where do you need Service Application improvement?
<--- Score

12. Do you have the optimal project management team structure?
<--- Score

13. Service Application risk decisions: whose call Is It?
<--- Score

14. Who makes the Service Application decisions in your organization?
<--- Score

15. What went well, what should change, what can improve?
<--- Score

16. What is the risk?
<--- Score

17. Can you identify any significant risks or exposures to Service Application third- parties (vendors, service providers, alliance partners etc) that concern you?
<--- Score

18. Where do the Service Application decisions reside?
<--- Score

19. Which Service Application solution is appropriate?
<--- Score

20. For decision problems, how do you develop a decision statement?
<--- Score

21. Is risk periodically assessed?
<--- Score

22. How do you manage Service Application risk?
<--- Score

23. How significant is the improvement in the eyes of the end user?
<--- Score

24. What are the Service Application security risks?
<--- Score

25. What are the implications of the one critical Service Application decision 10 minutes, 10 months, and 10 years from now?
<--- Score

26. Which of the recognised risks out of all risks can be most likely transferred?
<--- Score

27. What Service Application improvements can be made?
<--- Score

28. How will you measure the results?
<--- Score

29. How do you manage and improve your Service Application work systems to deliver customer value and achieve organizational success and sustainability?
<--- Score

30. How do the Service Application results compare with the performance of your competitors and other organizations with similar offerings?
<--- Score

31. How risky is your organization?
<--- Score

32. Who are the key stakeholders for the Service Application evaluation?
<--- Score

33. How can you better manage risk?
<--- Score

34. What risks do you need to manage?
<--- Score

35. What are the affordable Service Application risks?
<--- Score

36. Do you cover the five essential competencies: Communication, Collaboration,Innovation, Adaptability, and Leadership that improve an organizations ability to leverage the new Service Application in a volatile global economy?
<--- Score

37. Who controls key decisions that will be made?
<--- Score

38. Are decisions made in a timely manner?
<--- Score

39. Who will be responsible for making the decisions to include or exclude requested changes once Service Application is underway?
<--- Score

40. Who will be using the results of the measurement activities?
<--- Score

41. What were the underlying assumptions on the cost-benefit analysis?
<--- Score

42. How are policy decisions made and where?

<--- Score

43. Who are the Service Application decision-makers?
<--- Score

44. What do you want to improve?
<--- Score

45. Is the scope clearly documented?
<--- Score

46. What is the implementation plan?
<--- Score

47. Is the solution technically practical?
<--- Score

48. In the past few months, what is the smallest change you have made that has had the biggest positive result? What was it about that small change that produced the large return?
<--- Score

49. Who are the Service Application decision makers?
<--- Score

50. Do you combine technical expertise with business knowledge and Service Application Key topics include lifecycles, development approaches, requirements and how to make a business case?
<--- Score

51. What are the concrete Service Application results?
<--- Score

52. Are the risks fully understood, reasonable and

manageable?
<--- Score

53. Do you need to do a usability evaluation?
<--- Score

54. Is supporting Service Application documentation required?
<--- Score

55. What can you do to improve?
<--- Score

56. Who do you report Service Application results to?
<--- Score

57. Can the solution be designed and implemented within an acceptable time period?
<--- Score

58. How can you improve Service Application?
<--- Score

59. Do vendor agreements bring new compliance risk ?
<--- Score

60. At what point will vulnerability assessments be performed once Service Application is put into production (e.g., ongoing Risk Management after implementation)?
<--- Score

61. Have you identified breakpoints and/or risk tolerances that will trigger broad consideration of a potential need for intervention or modification of

strategy?
<--- Score

62. What tools were used to evaluate the potential solutions?
<--- Score

63. How will you know that you have improved?
<--- Score

64. How will you know that a change is an improvement?
<--- Score

65. Are the most efficient solutions problem-specific?
<--- Score

66. How does the team improve its work?
<--- Score

67. Are risk management tasks balanced centrally and locally?
<--- Score

68. What strategies for Service Application improvement are successful?
<--- Score

69. Does the goal represent a desired result that can be measured?
<--- Score

70. Do those selected for the Service Application team have a good general understanding of what Service Application is all about?
<--- Score

71. Was a Service Application charter developed?
<--- Score

72. Will the controls trigger any other risks?
<--- Score

73. How do you keep improving Service Application?
<--- Score

74. How can skill-level changes improve Service Application?
<--- Score

75. What is Service Application risk?
<--- Score

76. What assumptions are made about the solution and approach?
<--- Score

77. Is Service Application documentation maintained?
<--- Score

78. What improvements have been achieved?
<--- Score

79. What to do with the results or outcomes of measurements?
<--- Score

80. Have you achieved Service Application improvements?
<--- Score

81. What resources are required for the improvement

efforts?
<--- Score

82. Risk Identification: What are the possible risk events your organization faces in relation to Service Application?
<--- Score

83. What needs improvement? Why?
<--- Score

84. Is the Service Application documentation thorough?
<--- Score

85. What area needs the greatest improvement?
<--- Score

86. When you map the key players in your own work and the types/domains of relationships with them, which relationships do you find easy and which challenging, and why?
<--- Score

87. Who are the people involved in developing and implementing Service Application?
<--- Score

88. What lessons, if any, from a pilot were incorporated into the design of the full-scale solution?
<--- Score

89. Are procedures documented for managing Service Application risks?
<--- Score

90. What actually has to improve and by how much?
<--- Score

91. Is the measure of success for Service Application understandable to a variety of people?
<--- Score

92. How will you know when its improved?
<--- Score

93. Is the Service Application risk managed?
<--- Score

94. How do you go about comparing Service Application approaches/solutions?
<--- Score

95. How do you link measurement and risk?
<--- Score

96. To what extent does management recognize Service Application as a tool to increase the results?
<--- Score

97. What is the magnitude of the improvements?
<--- Score

98. What were the criteria for evaluating a Service Application pilot?
<--- Score

99. Risk events: what are the things that could go wrong?
<--- Score

100. How do you define the solutions' scope?

<--- Score

101. What is Service Application's impact on utilizing the best solution(s)?
<--- Score

102. How is knowledge sharing about risk management improved?
<--- Score

103. What tools were used to tap into the creativity and encourage 'outside the box' thinking?
<--- Score

104. Are you assessing Service Application and risk?
<--- Score

105. Are risk triggers captured?
<--- Score

106. What current systems have to be understood and/or changed?
<--- Score

107. Who manages Service Application risk?
<--- Score

108. Who manages supplier risk management in your organization?
<--- Score

109. Who will be responsible for documenting the Service Application requirements in detail?
<--- Score

110. How are Service Application risks managed?

<--- Score

111. Would you develop a Service Application Communication Strategy?
<--- Score

112. Are events managed to resolution?
<--- Score

113. How do you improve Service Application service perception, and satisfaction?
<--- Score

114. Can you integrate quality management and risk management?
<--- Score

115. What criteria will you use to assess your Service Application risks?
<--- Score

116. Are the key business and technology risks being managed?
<--- Score

117. Explorations of the frontiers of Service Application will help you build influence, improve Service Application, optimize decision making, and sustain change, what is your approach?
<--- Score

118. How does your organization evaluate strategic Service Application success?
<--- Score

119. For estimation problems, how do you develop an

estimation statement?

<--- Score

120. How do you measure improved Service Application service perception, and satisfaction?

<--- Score

121. How do you improve productivity?

<--- Score

122. What tools were most useful during the improve phase?

<--- Score

123. Does a good decision guarantee a good outcome?

<--- Score

124. How is continuous improvement applied to risk management?

<--- Score

125. What practices helps your organization to develop its capacity to recognize patterns?

<--- Score

126. How scalable is your Service Application solution?

<--- Score

127. How do you improve your likelihood of success ?

<--- Score

128. Is any Service Application documentation required?

<--- Score

129. Who should make the Service Application decisions?
<--- Score

130. If you could go back in time five years, what decision would you make differently? What is your best guess as to what decision you're making today you might regret five years from now?
<--- Score

131. How do you deal with Service Application risk?
<--- Score

132. How can the phases of Service Application development be identified?
<--- Score

133. Is there any other Service Application solution?
<--- Score

134. Risk factors: what are the characteristics of Service Application that make it risky?
<--- Score

Add up total points for this section:
_ _ _ _ _ = Total points for this section

Divided by: _ _ _ _ _ _ (number of statements answered) = _ _ _ _ _ _
Average score for this section

Transfer your score to the Service Application Index at the beginning of the Self-Assessment.

CRITERION #6: CONTROL:

INTENT: Implement the practical solution. Maintain the performance and correct possible complications.

In my belief, the answer to this question is clearly defined:

5 Strongly Agree

4 Agree

3 Neutral

2 Disagree

1 Strongly Disagree

1. Are there documented procedures?
<--- Score

2. How might the group capture best practices and lessons learned so as to leverage improvements?
<--- Score

3. Is there a transfer of ownership and knowledge to process owner and process team tasked with the

responsibilities.
<--- Score

4. Are controls in place and consistently applied?
<--- Score

5. How will new or emerging customer needs/
requirements be checked/communicated to orient
the process toward meeting the new specifications
and continually reducing variation?
<--- Score

6. What is your plan to assess your security risks?
<--- Score

7. What are the key elements of your Service
Application performance improvement system,
including your evaluation, organizational learning,
and innovation processes?
<--- Score

8. Are new process steps, standards, and
documentation ingrained into normal operations?
<--- Score

9. Does Service Application appropriately measure
and monitor risk?
<--- Score

10. How do you establish and deploy modified action
plans if circumstances require a shift in plans and
rapid execution of new plans?
<--- Score

11. Implementation Planning: is a pilot needed to test
the changes before a full roll out occurs?

<--- Score

12. How will the day-to-day responsibilities for monitoring and continual improvement be transferred from the improvement team to the process owner?
<--- Score

13. How do you select, collect, align, and integrate Service Application data and information for tracking daily operations and overall organizational performance, including progress relative to strategic objectives and action plans?
<--- Score

14. How will the process owner verify improvement in present and future sigma levels, process capabilities?
<--- Score

15. How is Service Application project cost planned, managed, monitored?
<--- Score

16. How do you spread information?
<--- Score

17. What are customers monitoring?
<--- Score

18. Do you monitor the effectiveness of your Service Application activities?
<--- Score

19. What are the critical parameters to watch?
<--- Score

20. What is the best design framework for Service Application organization now that, in a post industrial-age if the top-down, command and control model is no longer relevant?
<--- Score

21. Are documented procedures clear and easy to follow for the operators?
<--- Score

22. Who sets the Service Application standards?
<--- Score

23. What are the performance and scale of the Service Application tools?
<--- Score

24. What other areas of the group might benefit from the Service Application team's improvements, knowledge, and learning?
<--- Score

25. How do your controls stack up?
<--- Score

26. Will any special training be provided for results interpretation?
<--- Score

27. What are you attempting to measure/monitor?
<--- Score

28. How can you best use all of your knowledge repositories to enhance learning and sharing?
<--- Score

29. Is the Service Application test/monitoring cost justified?
<--- Score

30. Will the team be available to assist members in planning investigations?
<--- Score

31. Will existing staff require re-training, for example, to learn new business processes?
<--- Score

32. What should the next improvement project be that is related to Service Application?
<--- Score

33. Is a response plan established and deployed?
<--- Score

34. Does the Service Application performance meet the customer's requirements?
<--- Score

35. What quality tools were useful in the control phase?
<--- Score

36. What Service Application standards are applicable?
<--- Score

37. Does the response plan contain a definite closed loop continual improvement scheme (e.g., plan-do-check-act)?
<--- Score

38. What do your reports reflect?
<--- Score

39. Are suggested corrective/restorative actions indicated on the response plan for known causes to problems that might surface?
<--- Score

40. What is the recommended frequency of auditing?
<--- Score

41. Is a response plan in place for when the input, process, or output measures indicate an 'out-of-control' condition?
<--- Score

42. Are the Service Application standards challenging?
<--- Score

43. What other systems, operations, processes, and infrastructures (hiring practices, staffing, training, incentives/rewards, metrics/dashboards/scorecards, etc.) need updates, additions, changes, or deletions in order to facilitate knowledge transfer and improvements?
<--- Score

44. You may have created your quality measures at a time when you lacked resources, technology wasn't up to the required standard, or low service levels were the industry norm. Have those circumstances changed?
<--- Score

45. Is there a recommended audit plan for routine surveillance inspections of Service Application's

gains?

<--- Score

46. Is new knowledge gained imbedded in the response plan?

<--- Score

47. What do you measure to verify effectiveness gains?

<--- Score

48. Is there a standardized process?

<--- Score

49. Does job training on the documented procedures need to be part of the process team's education and training?

<--- Score

50. How will report readings be checked to effectively monitor performance?

<--- Score

51. What is your theory of human motivation, and how does your compensation plan fit with that view?

<--- Score

52. Can you adapt and adjust to changing Service Application situations?

<--- Score

53. How do you plan for the cost of succession?

<--- Score

54. What key inputs and outputs are being measured on an ongoing basis?

<--- Score

55. Act/Adjust: What Do you Need to Do Differently?
<--- Score

56. How widespread is its use?
<--- Score

57. Has the improved process and its steps been standardized?
<--- Score

58. Are operating procedures consistent?
<--- Score

59. Against what alternative is success being measured?
<--- Score

60. Does a troubleshooting guide exist or is it needed?
<--- Score

61. In the case of a Service Application project, the criteria for the audit derive from implementation objectives, an audit of a Service Application project involves assessing whether the recommendations outlined for implementation have been met, can you track that any Service Application project is implemented as planned, and is it working?
<--- Score

62. What adjustments to the strategies are needed?
<--- Score

63. How do controls support value?
<--- Score

64. Who has control over resources?
<--- Score

65. How do you encourage people to take control and responsibility?
<--- Score

66. Are the planned controls working?
<--- Score

67. Is there a Service Application Communication plan covering who needs to get what information when?
<--- Score

68. What is the standard for acceptable Service Application performance?
<--- Score

69. How is change control managed?
<--- Score

70. What are your results for key measures or indicators of the accomplishment of your Service Application strategy and action plans, including building and strengthening core competencies?
<--- Score

71. Who controls critical resources?
<--- Score

72. What can you control?
<--- Score

73. Is there an action plan in case of emergencies?
<--- Score

74. How do you plan on providing proper recognition and disclosure of supporting companies?
<--- Score

75. Is there documentation that will support the successful operation of the improvement?
<--- Score

76. How do senior leaders actions reflect a commitment to the organizations Service Application values?
<--- Score

77. Is reporting being used or needed?
<--- Score

78. How do you monitor usage and cost?
<--- Score

79. What are the known security controls?
<--- Score

80. Who will be in control?
<--- Score

81. Where do ideas that reach policy makers and planners as proposals for Service Application strengthening and reform actually originate?
<--- Score

82. Are you measuring, monitoring and predicting Service Application activities to optimize operations and profitability, and enhancing outcomes?
<--- Score

83. Do the viable solutions scale to future needs?
<--- Score

84. How will input, process, and output variables be checked to detect for sub-optimal conditions?
<--- Score

85. Is there a documented and implemented monitoring plan?
<--- Score

86. How will you measure your QA plan's effectiveness?
<--- Score

87. Is knowledge gained on process shared and institutionalized?
<--- Score

88. Have new or revised work instructions resulted?
<--- Score

89. Are pertinent alerts monitored, analyzed and distributed to appropriate personnel?
<--- Score

90. Can support from partners be adjusted?
<--- Score

91. What do you stand for--and what are you against?
<--- Score

92. Do you monitor the Service Application decisions made and fine tune them as they evolve?
<--- Score

93. What is the control/monitoring plan?
<--- Score

94. Who is the Service Application process owner?
<--- Score

95. What should you measure to verify efficiency gains?
<--- Score

96. How will the process owner and team be able to hold the gains?
<--- Score

97. Who is going to spread your message?
<--- Score

98. How likely is the current Service Application plan to come in on schedule or on budget?
<--- Score

99. Is there a control plan in place for sustaining improvements (short and long-term)?
<--- Score

Add up total points for this section:
_ _ _ _ _ = Total points for this section

Divided by: _ _ _ _ _ _ (number of statements answered) = _ _ _ _ _ _
Average score for this section

Transfer your score to the Service Application Index at the beginning of the Self-Assessment.

CRITERION #7: SUSTAIN:

INTENT: Retain the benefits.

In my belief, the answer to this question is clearly defined:

5 Strongly Agree

4 Agree

3 Neutral

2 Disagree

1 Strongly Disagree

1. Is your strategy driving your strategy? Or is the way in which you allocate resources driving your strategy? <--- Score

2. How do you lead with Service Application in mind? <--- Score

3. What happens if you do not have enough funding? <--- Score

4. What are specific Service Application rules to

follow?
<--- Score

5. Is it economical; do you have the time and money?
<--- Score

6. What role does communication play in the success or failure of a Service Application project?
<--- Score

7. Can the schedule be done in the given time?
<--- Score

8. How do you manage Service Application Knowledge Management (KM)?
<--- Score

9. Whom among your colleagues do you trust, and for what?
<--- Score

10. What are the rules and assumptions your industry operates under? What if the opposite were true?
<--- Score

11. Is your basic point _____ or _____?
<--- Score

12. Is the Service Application organization completing tasks effectively and efficiently?
<--- Score

13. What is the kind of project structure that would be appropriate for your Service Application project, should it be formal and complex, or can it be less formal and relatively simple?

<--- Score

14. In the past year, what have you done (or could you have done) to increase the accurate perception of your company/brand as ethical and honest?
<--- Score

15. How do you go about securing Service Application?
<--- Score

16. What trouble can you get into?
<--- Score

17. If you were responsible for initiating and implementing major changes in your organization, what steps might you take to ensure acceptance of those changes?
<--- Score

18. How are you engineering LaaS-service applications for this?
<--- Score

19. Are assumptions made in Service Application stated explicitly?
<--- Score

20. What are the business goals Service Application is aiming to achieve?
<--- Score

21. What are the long-term Service Application goals?
<--- Score

22. What are the gaps in your knowledge and

experience?
<--- Score

23. What should you stop doing?
<--- Score

24. How do you listen to customers to obtain actionable information?
<--- Score

25. Will it be accepted by users?
<--- Score

26. Who will provide the final approval of Service Application deliverables?
<--- Score

27. What is it like to work for you?
<--- Score

28. How do you keep the momentum going?
<--- Score

29. Can you do all this work?
<--- Score

30. What is the recommended frequency of auditing?
<--- Score

31. Who are the key stakeholders?
<--- Score

32. What is your competitive advantage?
<--- Score

33. What new services of functionality will be

implemented next with Service Application ?
<--- Score

34. What are the key enablers to make this Service Application move?
<--- Score

35. Why is it important to have senior management support for a Service Application project?
<--- Score

36. What are the success criteria that will indicate that Service Application objectives have been met and the benefits delivered?
<--- Score

37. Marketing budgets are tighter, consumers are more skeptical, and social media has changed forever the way we talk about Service Application, how do you gain traction?
<--- Score

38. How do you make it meaningful in connecting Service Application with what users do day-to-day?
<--- Score

39. What counts that you are not counting?
<--- Score

40. What are the top 3 things at the forefront of your Service Application agendas for the next 3 years?
<--- Score

41. In retrospect, of the projects that you pulled the plug on, what percent do you wish had been allowed to keep going, and what percent do you wish had

ended earlier?
<--- Score

42. Are the assumptions believable and achievable?
<--- Score

43. Operational - will it work?
<--- Score

44. Who do you think the world wants your organization to be?
<--- Score

45. How will you ensure you get what you expected?
<--- Score

46. To whom do you add value?
<--- Score

47. What are your personal philosophies regarding Service Application and how do they influence your work?
<--- Score

48. What is an unauthorized commitment?
<--- Score

49. Which individuals, teams or departments will be involved in Service Application?
<--- Score

50. Why is Service Application important for you now?
<--- Score

51. What have you done to protect your business from competitive encroachment?

<--- Score

52. Who is responsible for ensuring appropriate resources (time, people and money) are allocated to Service Application?
<--- Score

53. What trophy do you want on your mantle?
<--- Score

54. What is the purpose of Service Application in relation to the mission?
<--- Score

55. Is Service Application realistic, or are you setting yourself up for failure?
<--- Score

56. How do you ensure that implementations of Service Application products are done in a way that ensures safety?
<--- Score

57. Are the criteria for selecting recommendations stated?
<--- Score

58. What is the funding source for this project?
<--- Score

59. How are you engineering Augmented Reality-service applications for this?
<--- Score

60. Why will customers want to buy your organizations products/services?

<--- Score

61. How do you accomplish your long range Service Application goals?
<--- Score

62. What is the craziest thing you can do?
<--- Score

63. How do you transition from the baseline to the target?
<--- Score

64. What is the overall business strategy?
<--- Score

65. What business benefits will Service Application goals deliver if achieved?
<--- Score

66. What must you excel at?
<--- Score

67. Think of your Service Application project, what are the main functions?
<--- Score

68. Why not do Service Application?
<--- Score

69. Who do you want your customers to become?
<--- Score

70. What information is critical to your organization that your executives are ignoring?
<--- Score

71. How do you decide how much to remunerate an employee?
<--- Score

72. What would you recommend your friend do if he/she were facing this dilemma?
<--- Score

73. In a project to restructure Service Application outcomes, which stakeholders would you involve?
<--- Score

74. How do you create buy-in?
<--- Score

75. Instead of going to current contacts for new ideas, what if you reconnected with dormant contacts-- the people you used to know? If you were going reactivate a dormant tie, who would it be?
<--- Score

76. What Service Application skills are most important?
<--- Score

77. Where can you break convention?
<--- Score

78. Are all key stakeholders present at all Structured Walkthroughs?
<--- Score

79. How do you keep records, of what?
<--- Score

80. Who do we want your customers to become?
<--- Score

81. What happens at your organization when people fail?
<--- Score

82. What is the source of the strategies for Service Application strengthening and reform?
<--- Score

83. How will you motivate the stakeholders with the least vested interest?
<--- Score

84. What have been your experiences in defining long range Service Application goals?
<--- Score

85. Who, on the executive team or the board, has spoken to a customer recently?
<--- Score

86. How do you determine the key elements that affect Service Application workforce satisfaction, how are these elements determined for different workforce groups and segments?
<--- Score

87. How are you doing compared to your industry?
<--- Score

88. What could happen if you do not do it?
<--- Score

89. How do you maintain Service Application's

Integrity?
<--- Score

90. What are the short and long-term Service Application goals?
<--- Score

91. Do you think you know, or do you know you know ?
<--- Score

92. Who are four people whose careers you have enhanced?
<--- Score

93. Is Service Application dependent on the successful delivery of a current project?
<--- Score

94. Is a Service Application team work effort in place?
<--- Score

95. Why should people listen to you?
<--- Score

96. Who is responsible for Service Application?
<--- Score

97. What is your Service Application strategy?
<--- Score

98. Are you making progress, and are you making progress as Service Application leaders?
<--- Score

99. Do you have past Service Application successes?

<--- Score

100. How do you foster the skills, knowledge, talents, attributes, and characteristics you want to have?
<--- Score

101. What is the estimated value of the project?
<--- Score

102. What are strategies for increasing support and reducing opposition?
<--- Score

103. How will you know that the Service Application project has been successful?
<--- Score

104. Do you feel that more should be done in the Service Application area?
<--- Score

105. How do you track customer value, profitability or financial return, organizational success, and sustainability?
<--- Score

106. Which models, tools and techniques are necessary?
<--- Score

107. What was the last experiment you ran?
<--- Score

108. What unique value proposition (UVP) do you offer?
<--- Score

109. What relationships among Service Application trends do you perceive?
<--- Score

110. Who is responsible for errors?
<--- Score

111. What would have to be true for the option on the table to be the best possible choice?
<--- Score

112. What projects are going on in the organization today, and what resources are those projects using from the resource pools?
<--- Score

113. Are you maintaining a past–present–future perspective throughout the Service Application discussion?
<--- Score

114. Who will determine interim and final deadlines?
<--- Score

115. What happens when a new employee joins the organization?
<--- Score

116. What are internal and external Service Application relations?
<--- Score

117. If you do not follow, then how to lead?
<--- Score

118. What you are going to do to affect the numbers?
<--- Score

119. How do customers see your organization?
<--- Score

120. What is your formula for success in Service Application ?
<--- Score

121. What is the range of capabilities?
<--- Score

122. What one word do you want to own in the minds of your customers, employees, and partners?
<--- Score

123. What are you challenging?
<--- Score

124. Ask yourself: how would you do this work if you only had one staff member to do it?
<--- Score

125. How long will it take to change?
<--- Score

126. Who have you, as a company, historically been when you've been at your best?
<--- Score

127. What will be the consequences to the stakeholder (financial, reputation etc) if Service Application does not go ahead or fails to deliver the objectives?
<--- Score

128. What are current Service Application paradigms?
<--- Score

129. What management system can you use to leverage the Service Application experience, ideas, and concerns of the people closest to the work to be done?
<--- Score

130. Is there any existing Service Application governance structure?
<--- Score

131. Will there be any necessary staff changes (redundancies or new hires)?
<--- Score

132. Who will be responsible for deciding whether Service Application goes ahead or not after the initial investigations?
<--- Score

133. How do you set Service Application stretch targets and how do you get people to not only participate in setting these stretch targets but also that they strive to achieve these?
<--- Score

134. How do you engage the workforce, in addition to satisfying them?
<--- Score

135. How will you insure seamless interoperability of Service Application moving forward?
<--- Score

136. Who are your customers?
<--- Score

137. Is there any reason to believe the opposite of my current belief?
<--- Score

138. How do senior leaders deploy your organizations vision and values through your leadership system, to the workforce, to key suppliers and partners, and to customers and other stakeholders, as appropriate?
<--- Score

139. Which Service Application goals are the most important?
<--- Score

140. Do you think Service Application accomplishes the goals you expect it to accomplish?
<--- Score

141. Which functions and people interact with the supplier and or customer?
<--- Score

142. How do you govern and fulfill your societal responsibilities?
<--- Score

143. Why do and why don't your customers like your organization?
<--- Score

144. Is maximizing Service Application protection the same as minimizing Service Application loss?

<--- Score

145. Who else should you help?
<--- Score

146. What Service Application modifications can you make work for you?
<--- Score

147. How is implementation research currently incorporated into each of your goals?
<--- Score

148. When information truly is ubiquitous, when reach and connectivity are completely global, when computing resources are infinite, and when a whole new set of impossibilities are not only possible, but happening, what will that do to your business?
<--- Score

149. What are the challenges?
<--- Score

150. Can you maintain your growth without detracting from the factors that have contributed to your success?
<--- Score

151. Who uses your product in ways you never expected?
<--- Score

152. What are the potential basics of Service Application fraud?
<--- Score

153. What are your most important goals for the strategic Service Application objectives?
<--- Score

154. How important is Service Application to the user organizations mission?
<--- Score

155. If you find that you havent accomplished one of the goals for one of the steps of the Service Application strategy, what will you do to fix it?
<--- Score

156. What knowledge, skills and characteristics mark a good Service Application project manager?
<--- Score

157. At what moment would you think; Will I get fired?
<--- Score

158. What may be the consequences for the performance of an organization if all stakeholders are not consulted regarding Service Application?
<--- Score

159. Political -is anyone trying to undermine this project?
<--- Score

160. What is your question? Why?
<--- Score

161. What is the overall talent health of your organization as a whole at senior levels, and for each organization reporting to a member of the Senior Leadership Team?

<--- Score

162. Who is the main stakeholder, with ultimate responsibility for driving Service Application forward?
<--- Score

163. What potential megatrends could make your business model obsolete?
<--- Score

164. What is your BATNA (best alternative to a negotiated agreement)?
<--- Score

165. Are you / should you be revolutionary or evolutionary?
<--- Score

166. How can you incorporate support to ensure safe and effective use of Service Application into the services that you provide?
<--- Score

167. Would you rather sell to knowledgeable and informed customers or to uninformed customers?
<--- Score

168. What is something you believe that nearly no one agrees with you on?
<--- Score

169. What stupid rule would you most like to kill?
<--- Score

Add up total points for this section:
_ _ _ _ _ = Total points for this section

Divided by: _____ (number of
statements answered) = _____
Average score for this section

Transfer your score to the Service
Application Index at the beginning of
the Self-Assessment.

Service Application and Managing Projects, Criteria for Project Managers:

1.0 Initiating Process Group: Service Application

1. What communication items need improvement?

2. Are the Service Application project team and stakeholders meeting regularly and using a meeting agenda and taking notes to accurately document what is being covered and what happened in the weekly meetings?

3. Are the changes in your Service Application project being formally requested, analyzed, and approved by the appropriate decision makers?

4. Do you understand all business (operational), technical, resource and vendor risks associated with the Service Application project?

5. Do you understand the quality and control criteria that must be achieved for successful Service Application project completion?

6. What are the short and long term implications?

7. Where must it be done?

8. How will it affect me?

9. Will the Service Application project meet the client requirements, and will it achieve the business success criteria that justified doing the Service Application project in the first place?

10. Does it make any difference if you am successful?

11. What technical work to do in each phase?

12. The process to Manage Stakeholders is part of which process group?

13. Who is funding the Service Application project?

14. Are identified risks being monitored properly, are new risks arising during the Service Application project or are foreseen risks occurring?

15. Are stakeholders properly informed about the status of the Service Application project?

16. Are there resources to maintain and support the outcome of the Service Application project?

17. When must it be done?

18. How will you know you did it?

19. Professionals want to know what is expected from them what are the deliverables?

1.1 Project Charter: Service Application

20. Why Outsource?

21. What date will the task finish?

22. What are the assigned resources?

23. Name and describe the elements that deal with providing the detail?

24. Strategic fit: what is the strategic initiative identifier for this Service Application project?

25. What barriers do you predict to your success?

26. What are you trying to accomplish?

27. Service Application project background: what is the primary motivation for this Service Application project?

28. Who is the Service Application project Manager?

29. Is it an improvement over existing products?

30. Why have you chosen the aim you have set forth?

31. What are the constraints?

32. Why do you need to manage scope?

33. Who ise input and support will this Service Application project require?

34. Are there special technology requirements?

35. Who are the stakeholders?

36. Run it as as a startup?

37. Why the improvements?

38. Why is a Service Application project Charter used?

39. Fit with other Products Compliments – Cannibalizes?

1.2 Stakeholder Register: Service Application

40. How will reports be created?

41. What & Why?

42. How should employers make voices heard?

43. What are the major Service Application project milestones requiring communications or providing communications opportunities?

44. Is your organization ready for change?

45. What opportunities exist to provide communications?

46. Who wants to talk about Security?

47. Who is managing stakeholder engagement?

48. How big is the gap?

49. How much influence do they have on the Service Application project?

50. What is the power of the stakeholder?

1.3 Stakeholder Analysis Matrix: Service Application

51. Who will promote/support the Service Application project, provided that they are involved?

52. Who will be responsible for managing the outcome?

53. What is the relationship among stakeholders?

54. How can you fill the need to show progress?

55. Timescales, deadlines and pressures?

56. What tools would help you communicate?

57. New technologies, services, ideas?

58. Who is most interested in information about the topic and/or has previously initiated interest?

59. Who are potential allies and opponents?

60. How do you manage Service Application project Risk?

61. Own known vulnerabilities?

62. Why do you care?

63. Seasonality, weather effects?

64. New markets, vertical, horizontal?

65. Who is influential in the Service Application project area (both thematic and geographic areas)?

66. What is the stakeholders power and status in relation to the Service Application project?

67. How are you predicting what future (work)loads will be?

68. Insurmountable weaknesses?

69. Are there different rules or organizational models for men and women?

2.0 Planning Process Group: Service Application

70. Mitigate. what will you do to minimize the impact should a risk event occur?

71. What input will you be required to provide the Service Application project team?

72. How many days can task X be late in starting without affecting the Service Application project completion date?

73. If action is called for, what form should it take?

74. When will the Service Application project be done?

75. What is the NEXT thing to do?

76. To what extent is the program helping to influence your organizations policy framework?

77. When developing the estimates for Service Application project phases, you choose to add the individual estimates for the activities that comprise each phase. What type of estimation method are you using?

78. To what extent have the target population and participants made the activities own, taking an active role in it?

79. Are there efficient coordination mechanisms to avoid overloading the counterparts, participating stakeholders?

80. How well did the chosen processes fit the needs of the Service Application project?

81. Who are the Service Application project stakeholders?

82. How will you do it?

83. Did the program design/ implementation strategy adequately address the planning stage necessary to set up structures, hire staff etc.?

84. To what extent and in what ways are the Service Application project contributing to progress towards organizational reform?

85. If a risk event occurs, what will you do?

86. How are it Service Application projects different?

87. On which process should team members spend the most time?

88. To what extent has a PMO contributed to raising the quality of the design of the Service Application project?

2.1 Project Management Plan: Service Application

89. Who is the Service Application project Manager?

90. What went wrong?

91. When is the Service Application project management plan created?

92. If the Service Application project management plan is a comprehensive document that guides you in Service Application project execution and control, then what should it NOT contain?

93. Is there anything you would now do differently on your Service Application project based on past experience?

94. Has the selected plan been formulated using cost effectiveness and incremental analysis techniques?

95. What is the justification?

96. How well are you able to manage your risk?

97. Who manages integration?

98. Why do you manage integration?

99. Are alternatives safe, functional, constructible, economical, reasonable and sustainable?

100. Do the proposed changes from the Service Application project include any significant risks to safety?

101. Are calculations and results of analyzes essentially correct?

102. Was the peer (technical) review of the cost estimates duly coordinated with the cost estimate center of expertise and addressed in the review documentation and certification?

103. Is the appropriate plan selected based on your organizations objectives and evaluation criteria expressed in Principles and Guidelines policies?

104. What are the known stakeholder requirements?

105. What are the deliverables?

106. How can you best help your organization to develop consistent practices in Service Application project management planning stages?

107. Are there any scope changes proposed for a previously authorized Service Application project?

2.2 Scope Management Plan: Service Application

108. Is a pmo (Service Application project management office) in place and provide oversight to the Service Application project?

109. Is there any form of automated support for Issues Management?

110. Does the Service Application project have a Quality Culture?

111. Time estimation – how much time will be needed?

112. Is there an on-going process in place to monitor Service Application project risks?

113. Are adequate resources provided for the quality assurance function?

114. How many changes are you making?

115. Were Service Application project team members involved in the development of activity & task decomposition?

116. Have reserves been created to address risks?

117. Materials available for performing the work?

118. Do all stakeholders know how to access this

repository and where to find the Service Application project documentation?

119. Does the resource management plan include a personnel development plan?

120. Are the people assigned to the Service Application project sufficiently qualified?

121. Have key stakeholders been identified?

122. Are software metrics formally captured, analyzed and used as a basis for other Service Application project estimates?

123. Is it possible to track all classes of Service Application project work (e.g. scheduled, un-scheduled, defect repair, etc.)?

124. Has a resource management plan been created?

125. Will the Service Application project deliverables become accepted in writing?

126. How do you know when you are finished?

127. Is an industry recognized mechanized support tool(s) being used for Service Application project scheduling & tracking?

2.3 Requirements Management Plan: Service Application

128. Is the user satisfied?

129. Is there formal agreement on who has authority to request a change in requirements?

130. Do you know which stakeholders will participate in the requirements effort?

131. When and how will a requirements baseline be established in this Service Application project?

132. Who has the authority to reject Service Application project requirements?

133. What is a problem?

134. Who is responsible for quantifying the Service Application project requirements?

135. How knowledgeable is the team in the proposed application area?

136. Will you use tracing to help understand the impact of a change in requirements?

137. Describe the process for rejecting the Service Application project requirements. Who has the authority to reject Service Application project requirements?

138. Are all the stakeholders ready for the transition into the user community?

139. How will unresolved questions be handled once approval has been obtained?

140. Who will finally present the work or product(s) for acceptance?

141. In case of software development; Should you have a test for each code module?

142. Did you use declarative statements?

143. Do you have an appropriate arrangement for meetings?

144. Does the Service Application project have a Change Control process?

145. Did you provide clear and concise specifications?

146. If it exists, where is it housed?

147. Will you have access to stakeholders when you need them?

2.4 Requirements Documentation: Service Application

148. Consistency. are there any requirements conflicts?

149. What if the system wasn t implemented?

150. How linear / iterative is your Requirements Gathering process (or will it be)?

151. What is your Elevator Speech?

152. Have the benefits identified with the system being identified clearly?

153. What is the risk associated with cost and schedule?

154. What will be the integration problems?

155. Do technical resources exist?

156. Verifiability. can the requirements be checked?

157. What is a show stopper in the requirements?

158. Is the requirement realistically testable?

159. How can you document system requirements?

160. Can the requirements be checked?

161. What happens when requirements are wrong?

162. Are all functions required by the customer included?

163. Who provides requirements?

164. Does the system provide the functions which best support the customers needs?

165. Completeness. are all functions required by the customer included?

166. Basic work/business process; high-level, what is being touched?

167. Can you check system requirements?

2.5 Requirements Traceability Matrix: Service Application

168. How will it affect the stakeholders personally in career?

169. What are the chronologies, contingencies, consequences, criteria?

170. What is the WBS?

171. Will you use a Requirements Traceability Matrix?

172. How do you manage scope?

173. Describe the process for approving requirements so they can be added to the traceability matrix and Service Application project work can be performed. Will the Service Application project requirements become approved in writing?

174. Is there a requirements traceability process in place?

175. Why do you manage scope?

176. How small is small enough?

177. Do you have a clear understanding of all subcontracts in place?

178. What percentage of Service Application projects are producing traceability matrices between

requirements and other work products?

179. Why use a WBS?

2.6 Project Scope Statement: Service Application

180. Elements that deal with providing the detail?

181. If there is an independent oversight contractor, have they signed off on the Service Application project Plan?

182. Is there a baseline plan against which to measure progress?

183. Is the change control process documented and on file?

184. Is the plan under configuration management?

185. Will the risk documents be filed?

186. Are there backup strategies for key members of the Service Application project?

187. Were potential customers involved early in the planning process?

188. Are there specific processes you will use to evaluate and approve/reject changes?

189. Is this process communicated to the customer and team members?

190. Is the Service Application project sponsor function identified and defined?

191. Where and how does the team fit within your organization structure?

192. What went right?

193. Has the Service Application project scope statement been reviewed as part of the baseline process?

194. Are there issues that could affect the existing requirements for the result, service, or product if the scope changes?

195. Will an issue form be in use?

196. Has a method and process for requirement tracking been developed?

197. Will you need a statement of work?

198. Is there a Change Management Board?

2.7 Assumption and Constraint Log: Service Application

199. Is there documentation of system capability requirements, data requirements, environment requirements, security requirements, and computer and hardware requirements?

200. What worked well?

201. Do the requirements meet the standards of correctness, completeness, consistency, accuracy, and readability?

202. Security analysis has access to information that is sanitized?

203. Do documented requirements exist for all critical components and areas, including technical, business, interfaces, performance, security and conversion requirements?

204. No superfluous information or marketing narrative?

205. Is there a Steering Committee in place?

206. Do you know what your customers expectations are regarding this process?

207. Does the document/deliverable meet all requirements (for example, statement of work) specific to this deliverable?

208. Is staff trained on the software technologies that are being used on the Service Application project?

209. Are there procedures in place to effectively manage interdependencies with other Service Application projects / systems?

210. Does the system design reflect the requirements?

211. How can you prevent/fix violations?

212. What if failure during recovery?

213. Are there standards for code development?

214. Are there nonconformance issues?

215. How do you design an auditing system?

216. Is this model reasonable?

217. Contradictory information between document sections?

218. What strengths do you have?

2.8 Work Breakdown Structure: Service Application

219. How many levels?

220. Is it a change in scope?

221. What has to be done?

222. Why is it useful?

223. When would you develop a Work Breakdown Structure?

224. How much detail?

225. Is the work breakdown structure (wbs) defined and is the scope of the Service Application project clear with assigned deliverable owners?

226. Is it still viable?

227. Where does it take place?

228. Can you make it?

229. Do you need another level?

230. When do you stop?

231. When does it have to be done?

232. How far down?

233. How will you and your Service Application project team define the Service Application projects scope and work breakdown structure?

234. What is the probability that the Service Application project duration will exceed xx weeks?

235. How big is a work-package?

2.9 WBS Dictionary: Service Application

236. All cwbs elements specified for external reporting?

237. Does the contractor have procedures which permit identification of recurring or non-recurring costs as necessary?

238. What should you drop in order to add something new?

239. Does the contractor use objective results, design reviews and tests to trace schedule performance?

240. Is each control account assigned to a single organizational element directly responsible for the work and identifiable to a single element of the CWBS?

241. Knowledgeable Service Application projections of future performance?

242. Are records maintained to show full accountability for all material purchased for the contract, including the residual inventory?

243. Are the latest revised estimates of costs at completion compared with the established budgets at appropriate levels and causes of variances identified?

244. Is all contract work included in the CWBS?

245. Are control accounts opened and closed based on the start and completion of work contained therein?

246. Time-phased control account budgets?

247. Contractor financial periods; for example, annual?

248. Are estimates of costs at completion utilized in determining contract funding requirements and reporting them?

249. Is budgeted cost for work performed calculated in a manner consistent with the way work is planned?

250. Does the contractors system provide for determination of price variance by comparing planned Vs actual commitments?

251. Wbs elements contractually specified for reporting of status to you (lowest level only)?

252. Are overhead cost budgets established for each organization which has authority to incur overhead costs?

253. Are authorized changes being incorporated in a timely manner?

254. Are your organizations and items of cost assigned to each pool identified?

2.10 Schedule Management Plan: Service Application

255. Does the ims include all contract and/or designated management control milestones?

256. Are corrective actions and variances reported?

257. Have the key elements of a coherent Service Application project management strategy been established?

258. Has a sponsor been identified?

259. What threats might prevent you from getting there?

260. What will be the final cost of the Service Application project if status quo is maintained?

261. Is the assigned Service Application project manager a PMP (Certified Service Application project manager) and experienced?

262. Is the critical path valid?

263. Is a process for scheduling and reporting defined, including forms and formats?

264. Are software metrics formally captured, analyzed and used as a basis for other Service Application project estimates?

265. Cost / benefit analysis?

266. Are the activity durations realistic and at an appropriate level of detail for effective management?

267. Has the ims content been baselined and is it adequately controlled?

268. Is the plan consistent with industry best practices?

269. Was the scope definition used in task sequencing?

270. Are right task and resource calendars used in the IMS?

271. Are target dates established for each milestone deliverable?

272. Is there a formal set of procedures supporting Issues Management?

273. Where is the scheduling tool and who has access to it to view it?

274. Are the Service Application project plans updated on a frequent basis?

2.11 Activity List: Service Application

275. Can you determine the activity that must finish, before this activity can start?

276. The wbs is developed as part of a joint planning session. and how do you know that youhave done this right?

277. What is the total time required to complete the Service Application project if no delays occur?

278. What will be performed?

279. Should you include sub-activities?

280. How detailed should a Service Application project get?

281. What is the probability the Service Application project can be completed in xx weeks?

282. How can the Service Application project be displayed graphically to better visualize the activities?

283. How much slack is available in the Service Application project?

284. What is your organizations history in doing similar activities?

285. Who will perform the work?

286. Are the required resources available or need to

be acquired?

287. What is the LF and LS for each activity?

288. How will it be performed?

289. What are the critical bottleneck activities?

290. How difficult will it be to do specific activities on this Service Application project?

291. How do you determine the late start (LS) for each activity?

292. When do the individual activities need to start and finish?

2.12 Activity Attributes: Service Application

293. Which method produces the more accurate cost assignment?

294. How else could the items be grouped?

295. Do you feel very comfortable with your prediction?

296. Are the required resources available?

297. Resource is assigned to?

298. Have constraints been applied to the start and finish milestones for the phases?

299. Resources to accomplish the work?

300. Has management defined a definite timeframe for the turnaround or Service Application project window?

301. Can you re-assign any activities to another resource to resolve an over-allocation?

302. Would you consider either of corresponding activities an outlier?

303. Can more resources be added?

304. Activity: what is In the Bag?

305. Where else does it apply?

306. What activity do you think you should spend the most time on?

307. How much activity detail is required?

308. Activity: what is Missing?

309. How many days do you need to complete the work scope with a limit of X number of resources?

310. What conclusions/generalizations can you draw from this?

2.13 Milestone List: Service Application

311. New USPs?

312. Describe your organizations strengths and core competencies. What factors will make your organization succeed?

313. What is the market for your technology, product or service?

314. Gaps in capabilities?

315. What specific improvements did you make to the Service Application project proposal since the previous time?

316. How late can the activity start?

317. Can you derive how soon can the whole Service Application project finish?

318. How will you get the word out to customers?

319. Describe the industry you are in and the market growth opportunities. What is the market for your technology, product or service?

320. Who will manage the Service Application project on a day-to-day basis?

321. Vital contracts and partners?

322. Effects on core activities, distraction?

323. How will the milestone be verified?

324. What has been done so far?

325. How soon can the activity finish?

326. Obstacles faced?

327. Reliability of data, plan predictability?

328. Which path is the critical path?

329. How late can each activity be finished and started?

2.14 Network Diagram: Service Application

330. If the Service Application project network diagram cannot change and you have extra personnel resources, what is the BEST thing to do?

331. Can you calculate the confidence level?

332. What are the Major Administrative Issues?

333. What is the completion time?

334. What can be done concurrently?

335. How confident can you be in your milestone dates and the delivery date?

336. Planning: who, how long, what to do?

337. What must be completed before an activity can be started?

338. Are the gantt chart and/or network diagram updated periodically and used to assess the overall Service Application project timetable?

339. What controls the start and finish of a job?

340. How difficult will it be to do specific activities on this Service Application project?

341. What activities must occur simultaneously with

this activity?

342. Which type of network diagram allows you to depict four types of dependencies?

343. What are the tools?

344. What job or jobs precede it?

345. Where do you schedule uncertainty time?

346. Exercise: what is the probability that the Service Application project duration will exceed xx weeks?

347. Will crashing x weeks return more in benefits than it costs?

348. What job or jobs could run concurrently?

2.15 Activity Resource Requirements: Service Application

349. Is there anything planned that does not need to be here?

350. Do you use tools like decomposition and rolling-wave planning to produce the activity list and other outputs?

351. Organizational Applicability?

352. Are there unresolved issues that need to be addressed?

353. Time for overtime?

354. How many signatures do you require on a check and does this match what is in your policy and procedures?

355. Which logical relationship does the PDM use most often?

356. How do you manage time?

357. Other support in specific areas?

358. How do you handle petty cash?

359. What is the Work Plan Standard?

360. What are constraints that you might find during

the Human Resource Planning process?

361. Why do you do that?

362. When does monitoring begin?

363. Anything else?

2.16 Resource Breakdown Structure: Service Application

364. What is the difference between % Complete and % work?

365. Who will be used as a Service Application project team member?

366. What is the primary purpose of the human resource plan?

367. What is each stakeholders desired outcome for the Service Application project?

368. Any changes from stakeholders?

369. Who delivers the information?

370. Why time management?

371. What defines a successful Service Application project?

372. Changes based on input from stakeholders?

373. Who will use the system?

374. How difficult will it be to do specific activities on this Service Application project?

375. Goals for the Service Application project. What is each stakeholders desired outcome for the Service

Application project?

376. Which resource planning tool provides information on resource responsibility and accountability?

377. How can this help you with team building?

378. How should the information be delivered?

379. Who needs what information?

2.17 Activity Duration Estimates: Service Application

380. Is training acquired to enhance the skills, knowledge and capabilities of the Service Application project team?

381. What is the career outlook for Service Application project managers in information technology?

382. How can software assist in procuring goods and services?

383. What should be done NEXT?

384. Service Application project manager is using weighted average duration estimates to perform schedule network analysis. Which type of mathematical analysis is being used?

385. What are the options you found to help people prepare for the exam?

386. Do your results resemble a normal distribution?

387. Is the Service Application project performing better or worse than planned?

388. Does a process exist to determine the probability of risk events?

389. What type of activity sequencing method is required for corresponding activities?

390. Will outside resources be needed to help in its development?

391. Are measurement techniques employed to determine the potential impact of proposed changes?

392. Can they use the already stated?

393. Who will provide training for the new application?

394. Are operational definitions created to identify quality measurement criteria for specific activities?

395. Account for the four frames of organizations. How can they help Service Application project managers understand your organizational context for Service Application projects?

396. Does a process exist to determine the potential loss or gain if risk events occur?

397. Is action taken to increase the effectiveness and efficiency of Service Application projects?

398. How difficult will it be to complete specific activities on this Service Application project?

2.18 Duration Estimating Worksheet: Service Application

399. Does the Service Application project provide innovative ways for stakeholders to overcome obstacles or deliver better outcomes?

400. How should ongoing costs be monitored to try to keep the Service Application project within budget?

401. When, then?

402. Do any colleagues have experience with your organization and/or RFPs?

403. Value pocket identification & quantification what are value pockets?

404. What is an Average Service Application project?

405. What is the total time required to complete the Service Application project if no delays occur?

406. What info is needed?

407. Will the Service Application project collaborate with the local community and leverage resources?

408. What utility impacts are there?

409. Small or large Service Application project?

410. When does your organization expect to be able

to complete it?

411. Is a construction detail attached (to aid in explanation)?

412. What work will be included in the Service Application project?

413. Why estimate time and cost?

414. Can the Service Application project be constructed as planned?

415. Define the work as completely as possible. What work will be included in the Service Application project?

416. Done before proceeding with this activity or what can be done concurrently?

2.19 Project Schedule: Service Application

417. Is the structure for tracking the Service Application project schedule well defined and assigned to a specific individual?

418. What is risk management?

419. Is there a Schedule Management Plan that establishes the criteria and activities for developing, monitoring and controlling the Service Application project schedule?

420. What is the most mis-scheduled part of process?

421. Are procedures defined by which the Service Application project schedule may be changed?

422. How do you know that youhave done this right?

423. Are quality inspections and review activities listed in the Service Application project schedule(s)?

424. Why is software Service Application project disaster so common?

425. Your Service Application project management plan results in a Service Application project schedule that is too long. If the Service Application project network diagram cannot change and you have extra personnel resources, what is the BEST thing to do?

426. Are all remaining durations correct?

427. Did the final product meet or exceed user expectations?

428. To what degree is do you feel the entire team was committed to the Service Application project schedule?

429. Schedule/cost recovery?

430. Why or why not?

431. How can you shorten the schedule?

432. Understand the constraints used in preparing the schedule. Are activities connected because logic dictates the order in which others occur?

433. How can you fix it?

434. Should you have a test for each code module?

435. Verify that the update is accurate. Are all remaining durations correct?

2.20 Cost Management Plan: Service Application

436. Have activity relationships and interdependencies within tasks been adequately identified?

437. Cost management – how will the cost of changes be estimated and controlled?

438. Does the Service Application project have a Statement of Work?

439. What does this mean to a cost or scheduler manager?

440. What is Service Application project management?

441. Has a structured approach been used to break work effort into manageable components (WBS)?

442. Exclusions – is there scope to be performed or provided by others?

443. Similar Service Application projects?

444. Schedule contingency – how will the schedule contingency be administrated?

445. Service Application project Objectives?

446. Are meeting objectives identified for each

meeting?

447. Have stakeholder accountabilities & responsibilities been clearly defined?

448. Have the procedures for identifying budget variances been followed?

449. Are parking lot items captured?

450. Are Service Application project contact logs kept up to date?

451. Forecasts – how will the time and resources needed to complete the Service Application project be forecast?

452. Are changes in scope (deliverable commitments) agreed to by all affected groups & individuals?

453. Eac -estimate at completion, what is the total job expected to cost?

454. Were Service Application project team members involved in the development of activity & task decomposition?

455. Does the detailed work plan match the complexity of tasks with the capabilities of personnel?

2.21 Activity Cost Estimates: Service Application

456. Are data needed on characteristics of care?

457. Would you hire them again?

458. Will you need to provide essential services information about activities?

459. What do you want to know about the stay to know if costs were inappropriately high or low?

460. Does the estimator have experience?

461. What happens if you cannot produce the documentation for the single audit?

462. Who determines when the contractor is paid?

463. If you are asked to lower your estimate because the price is too high, what are your options?

464. Estimated cost?

465. Were escalated issues resolved promptly?

466. Can you delete activities or make them inactive?

467. Where can you get activity reports?

468. What are you looking for?

469. How difficult will it be to do specific tasks on the Service Application project?

470. Can you change your activities?

471. What were things that you did well, and could improve, and how?

472. How and when do you enter into Service Application project Procurement Management?

473. Did the Service Application project team have the right skills?

474. Who & what determines the need for contracted services?

2.22 Cost Estimating Worksheet: Service Application

475. What will others want?

476. Who is best positioned to know and assist in identifying corresponding factors?

477. Ask: are others positioned to know, are others credible, and will others cooperate?

478. Does the Service Application project provide innovative ways for stakeholders to overcome obstacles or deliver better outcomes?

479. Is the Service Application project responsive to community need?

480. What is the estimated labor cost today based upon this information?

481. What can be included?

482. Can a trend be established from historical performance data on the selected measure and are the criteria for using trend analysis or forecasting methods met?

483. What happens to any remaining funds not used?

484. What is the purpose of estimating?

485. Will the Service Application project collaborate

with the local community and leverage resources?

486. What additional Service Application project(s) could be initiated as a result of this Service Application project?

487. How will the results be shared and to whom?

488. Is it feasible to establish a control group arrangement?

489. What costs are to be estimated?

490. Identify the timeframe necessary to monitor progress and collect data to determine how the selected measure has changed?

2.23 Cost Baseline: Service Application

491. How fast?

492. How accurate do cost estimates need to be?

493. Will the Service Application project fail if the change request is not executed?

494. Have the lessons learned been filed with the Service Application project Management Office?

495. Is the requested change request a result of changes in other Service Application project(s)?

496. How difficult will it be to do specific tasks on the Service Application project?

497. Has the actual cost of the Service Application project (or Service Application project phase) been tallied and compared to the approved budget?

498. Has the documentation relating to operation and maintenance of the product(s) or service(s) been delivered to, and accepted by, operations management?

499. Vac -variance at completion, how much over/ under budget do you expect to be?

500. What does a good WBS NOT look like?

501. What do you want to measure ?

502. Review your risk triggers -have your risks changed?

503. Are you asking management for something as a result of this update?

504. Impact to environment?

505. What weaknesses do you have?

506. Is request in line with priorities?

507. Are there contingencies or conditions related to the acceptance?

2.24 Quality Management Plan: Service Application

508. Are formal code reviews conducted?

509. Is there a Quality Management Plan?

510. List your organizations customer contact standards that employees are expected to maintain. How are corresponding standards measured?

511. Are decisions/actions based on data collected?

512. Who is responsible?

513. Were there any deficiencies / issues identified in the prior years self-assessment?

514. What has the QM Collaboration done?

515. Do trained quality assurance auditors conduct the audits as defined in the Quality Management Plan and scheduled by the Service Application project manager?

516. Does a documented Service Application project organizational policy & plan (i.e. governance model) exist?

517. What else should you do now?

518. How are people conducting sampling trained?

519. How is equipment calibrated?

520. How do senior leaders create an environment that encourages learning and innovation?

521. Does the program conduct field testing?

522. How are calibration records kept?

523. Who gets results of work?

524. How are changes approved?

525. When reporting to different audiences, do you vary the form or type of report?

526. Who do you send data to?

2.25 Quality Metrics: Service Application

527. How do you know if everyone is trying to improve the right things?

528. What method of measurement do you use?

529. What metrics do you measure?

530. What are your organizations next steps?

531. Where is quality now?

532. What level of statistical confidence do you use?

533. What makes a visualization memorable?

534. How do you measure?

535. Why is now the time for quality metrics?

536. What if the biggest risk to your business were the already stated people who do not complain?

537. Are quality metrics defined?

538. Is quality culture a competitive advantage?

539. Is there a set of procedures to capture, analyze and act on quality metrics?

540. Filter visualizations of interest?

541. How should customers provide input?

542. Is material complete (and does it meet the standards)?

543. Is a risk containment plan in place?

544. What percentage are outcome-based?

2.26 Process Improvement Plan: Service Application

545. Does your process ensure quality?

546. Modeling current processes is great, and will you ever see a return on that investment?

547. Has a process guide to collect the data been developed?

548. Has the time line required to move measurement results from the points of collection to databases or users been established?

549. Why quality management?

550. Are there forms and procedures to collect and record the data?

551. What personnel are the sponsors for that initiative?

552. Purpose of goal: the motive is determined by asking, why do you want to achieve this goal?

553. Are you making progress on the goals?

554. Have the supporting tools been developed or acquired?

555. What personnel are the champions for the initiative?

556. Are you following the quality standards?

557. The motive is determined by asking, Why do you want to achieve this goal?

558. Where are you now?

559. Are you meeting the quality standards?

560. How do you manage quality?

561. What is quality and how will you ensure it?

562. Have the frequency of collection and the points in the process where measurements will be made been determined?

563. What personnel are the change agents for your initiative?

2.27 Responsibility Assignment Matrix: Service Application

564. Who is the sponsor?

565. Identify and isolate causes of favorable and unfavorable cost and schedule variances?

566. What do you need to implement earned value management?

567. Identify potential or actual overruns and underruns?

568. Is the entire contract planned in time-phased control accounts to the extent practicable?

569. The anticipated business volume?

570. Is it safe to say you can handle more work or that some tasks you are supposed to do arent worth doing?

571. Does the scheduling system identify in a timely manner the status of work?

572. Does the Service Application project need to be analyzed further to uncover additional responsibilities?

573. No rs: if a task has no one listed as responsible, who is getting the job done?

574. Detailed schedules which support control account and work package start and completion dates/events?

575. What is the number one predictor of a groups productivity?

576. How do you assist them to be as productive as possible?

577. Are records maintained to show how management reserves are used?

578. Service Application projected economic escalation?

579. Do managers and team members provide helpful suggestions during review meetings?

580. Availability – will the group or the person be available within the necessary time interval?

2.28 Roles and Responsibilities: Service Application

581. Where are you most strong as a supervisor?

582. Influence: what areas of organizational decision making are you able to influence when you do not have authority to make the final decision?

583. Once the responsibilities are defined for the Service Application project, have the deliverables, roles and responsibilities been clearly communicated to every participant?

584. Is the data complete?

585. Once the responsibilities are defined for the Service Application project, have the deliverables, roles and responsibilities been clearly communicated to every participant?

586. Authority: what areas/Service Application projects in your work do you have the authority to decide upon and act on the already stated decisions?

587. What specific behaviors did you observe?

588. What expectations were met?

589. Are governance roles and responsibilities documented?

590. Who is responsible for each task?

591. What areas would you highlight for changes or improvements?

592. Be specific; avoid generalities. Thank you and great work alone are insufficient. What exactly do you appreciate and why?

593. What should you do now to prepare for your career 5+ years from now?

594. Concern: where are you limited or have no authority, where you can not influence?

595. Who: who is involved?

596. Implementation of actions: Who are the responsible units?

597. Are the quality assurance functions and related roles and responsibilities clearly defined?

598. Does your vision/mission support a culture of quality data?

599. Is there a training program in place for stakeholders covering expectations, roles and responsibilities and any addition knowledge others need to be good stakeholders?

600. Are Service Application project team roles and responsibilities identified and documented?

2.29 Human Resource Management Plan: Service Application

601. Is a payment system in place with proper reviews and approvals?

602. Are updated Service Application project time & resource estimates reasonable based on the current Service Application project stage?

603. Is the manpower level sufficient to meet the future business requirements?

604. Has the Service Application project scope been baselined?

605. Are the Service Application project team members located locally to the users/stakeholders?

606. Personnel with expertise?

607. Are Service Application project team members involved in detailed estimating and scheduling?

608. Has a capability assessment been conducted?

609. Are vendor contract reports, reviews and visits conducted periodically?

610. How will the Service Application project manage expectations & meet needs and requirements?

611. Measurable - are the targets measurable?

612. How well does your organization communicate?

613. Has the business need been clearly defined?

614. Is there an on-going process in place to monitor Service Application project risks?

615. Are risk triggers captured?

616. Responsiveness to change and the resulting demands for different skills and abilities?

617. Is an industry recognized support tool(s) being used for Service Application project scheduling & tracking?

2.30 Communications Management Plan: Service Application

618. What to learn?

619. Who is involved as you identify stakeholders?

620. Are stakeholders internal or external?

621. Is the stakeholder role recognized by your organization?

622. Which stakeholders can influence others?

623. Timing: when do the effects of the communication take place?

624. What is Service Application project communications management?

625. Who is the stakeholder?

626. Who will use or be affected by the result of a Service Application project?

627. What is the stakeholders level of authority?

628. Who are the members of the governing body?

629. What are the interrelationships?

630. How will the person responsible for executing the communication item be notified?

631. Is there an important stakeholder who is actively opposed and will not receive messages?

632. What does the stakeholder need from the team?

633. Do you prepare stakeholder engagement plans?

634. Why manage stakeholders?

635. Who were proponents/opponents?

636. How is this initiative related to other portfolios, programs, or Service Application projects?

637. Conflict resolution -which method when?

2.31 Risk Management Plan: Service Application

638. What is the probability the risk avoidance strategy will be successful?

639. Premium on reliability of product?

640. Are some people working on multiple Service Application projects?

641. Is the process being followed?

642. How do you manage Service Application project Risk?

643. Why do you want risk management?

644. Financial risk: can your organization afford to undertake the Service Application project?

645. Are there risks to human health or the environment that need to be controlled or mitigated?

646. Number of users of the product?

647. What would you do differently?

648. What risks are tracked?

649. How much risk protection can you afford?

650. People risk -are people with appropriate skills

available to help complete the Service Application project?

651. Are enough people available?

652. Are the software tools integrated with each other?

653. What are the cost, schedule and resource impacts of avoiding the risk?

654. Can the Service Application project proceed without assuming the risk?

655. Why is product liability a serious issue?

656. What will the damage be?

2.32 Risk Register: Service Application

657. What has changed since the last period?

658. Who needs to know about this?

659. What are you going to do to limit the Service Application projects risk exposure due to the identified risks?

660. What should you do now?

661. What further options might be available for responding to the risk?

662. What is the probability and impact of the risk occurring?

663. User involvement: do you have the right users?

664. Assume the event happens, what is the Most Likely impact?

665. Are there other alternative controls that could be implemented?

666. Manageability – have mitigations to the risk been identified?

667. Having taken action, how did the responses effect change, and where is the Service Application project now?

668. Which key risks have ineffective responses or

outstanding improvement actions?

669. Is further information required before making a decision?

670. People risk -are people with appropriate skills available to help complete the Service Application project?

671. What will be done?

672. Recovery actions - planned actions taken once a risk has occurred to allow you to move on. What should you do after?

673. When would you develop a risk register?

674. How are risks identified?

675. Methodology: how will risk management be performed on this Service Application project?

676. Budget and schedule: what are the estimated costs and schedules for performing risk-related activities?

2.33 Probability and Impact Assessment: Service Application

677. What should be the level of coordination?

678. What is the Service Application project managers level of commitment and professionalism?

679. Management -what contingency plans do you have if the risk becomes a reality?

680. Have decisions that should be left open because of inadequate information on technology been identified and responsibility assigned for reducing the uncertainty?

681. What will be the environmental impact of the Service Application project?

682. Do requirements put excessive performance constraints on the product?

683. Is the process supported by tools?

684. What are the chances the event will occur?

685. What are the chances the risk event will occur?

686. Which role do you have in the Service Application project?

687. Prioritized components/features?

688. Do you use any methods to analyze risks?

689. Are tool mentors available?

690. What should be the requirement of organizational restructuring as each subService Application project goes through a different lifecycle phase?

691. Will there be an increase in the political conservatism?

692. Supply/demand Service Application projections and trends; what are the levels of accuracy?

693. What can you do about it?

694. What kind of preparation would be required to do this?

695. Would avoiding any of corresponding impact the Service Application projects chance of success?

696. Is security a central objective?

2.34 Probability and Impact Matrix: Service Application

697. What will be the likely political environment during the life of the Service Application project?

698. Is the customer technically sophisticated in the product area?

699. What risks were tracked?

700. Who is going to be the consortium leader?

701. What will be the environmental impact of the Service Application project?

702. What did not work so well?

703. How to prioritize risks?

704. While preparing your risk responses, you identify additional risks. What should you do?

705. Is the customer willing to establish rapid communication links with the developer?

706. What is the likelihood of a breakthrough?

707. What are the uncertainties associated with the technology selected for the Service Application project?

708. Are some people working on multiple Service

Application projects?

709. How well were you able to manage your risk?

710. Are there new risks that mitigation strategies might introduce?

711. Is the present organizational structure for handling the Service Application project sufficient?

712. How will the consumption pattern change?

713. Are you working on the right risks?

714. Can the Service Application project proceed without assuming the risk?

2.35 Risk Data Sheet: Service Application

715. What do people affected think about the need for, and practicality of preventive measures?

716. Potential for recurrence?

717. What are your core values?

718. Type of risk identified?

719. What are the main threats to your existence?

720. Is the data sufficiently specified in terms of the type of failure being analyzed, and its frequency or probability?

721. Are new hazards created?

722. What will be the consequences if the risk happens?

723. What are you weak at and therefore need to do better?

724. During work activities could hazards exist?

725. What actions can be taken to eliminate or remove risk?

726. Whom do you serve (customers)?

727. What is the likelihood of it happening?

728. Who has a vested interest in how you perform as your organization (our stakeholders)?

729. What is the chance that it will happen?

730. Has a sensitivity analysis been carried out?

731. Do effective diagnostic tests exist?

732. What will be the consequences if it happens?

733. What are you trying to achieve (Objectives)?

2.36 Procurement Management Plan: Service Application

734. Are the Service Application project plans updated on a frequent basis?

735. Are Service Application project leaders committed to this Service Application project full time?

736. In which phase of the Acquisition Process Cycle does source qualifications reside?

737. Is documentation created for communication with the suppliers and Vendors?

738. Are all payments made according to the contract(s)?

739. Has the schedule been baselined?

740. Is there an approved case?

741. Are the quality tools and methods identified in the Quality Plan appropriate to the Service Application project?

742. Staffing Requirements?

743. Has the scope management document been updated and distributed to help prevent scope creep?

744. Financial capacity; does the seller have, or can

the seller reasonably be expected to obtain, the financial resources needed?

745. Does the business case include how the Service Application project aligns with your organizations strategic goals & objectives?

746. Are risk oriented checklists used during risk identification?

747. Are software metrics formally captured, analyzed and used as a basis for other Service Application project estimates?

748. Are Service Application project team members involved in detailed estimating and scheduling?

2.37 Source Selection Criteria: Service Application

749. What are the guiding principles for developing an evaluation report?

750. Have all evaluators been trained?

751. Do you ensure you evaluate what you asked for, not what you want to see or expect to see?

752. Is experience evaluated?

753. When must you conduct a debriefing?

754. What should be the contracting officers strategy?

755. Do you want to have them collaborate at subfactor level?

756. If the costs are normalized, please account for how the normalization is conducted. Is a cost realism analysis used?

757. How should the solicitation aspects regarding past performance be structured?

758. Is the offeror pricing what is technically proposed?

759. How will you evaluate offerors proposals?

760. How organization are proposed quotes/prices?

761. What can not be disclosed?

762. What is the role of counsel in the procurement process?

763. Who is entitled to a debriefing?

764. How should the preproposal conference be conducted?

765. Do proposed hours support content and schedule?

766. Does an evaluation need to include the identification of strengths and weaknesses?

767. Team leads: what is your process for assigning ratings?

768. How should the oral presentations be handled?

2.38 Stakeholder Management Plan: Service Application

769. Are the payment terms being followed?

770. Does the Service Application project have a Quality Culture?

771. Which risks pose the highest threat?

772. Are schedule deliverables actually delivered?

773. Will Service Application project success require up to date information at a moments notice?

774. Is the quality assurance team identified?

775. What are reporting requirements?

776. Are all vendor contracts closed out?

777. Are Service Application project team members involved in detailed estimating and scheduling?

778. Are best practices and metrics employed to identify issues, progress, performance, etc.?

779. Can the requirements be traced to the appropriate components of the solution, as well as test scripts?

780. Who is responsible for arranging and managing the review(s)?

781. Were the budget estimates reasonable?

782. Are all resource assumptions documented?

783. Are internal Service Application project status meetings held at reasonable intervals?

2.39 Change Management Plan: Service Application

784. How frequently should you repeat the message?

785. Who might present the most resistance?

786. Do you need a new organization structure?

787. What provokes organizational change?

788. Where do you want to be?

789. Clearly articulate the overall business benefits of the Service Application project -why are you doing this now?

790. When to start change management?

791. What relationships will change?

792. Will a different work structure focus people on what is important?

793. Who might be able to help you the most?

794. What is the reason for the communication?

795. How much change management is needed?

796. Who will do the training?

797. Has the target training audience been identified

and nominated?

798. How does the principle of senders and receivers make the Service Application project communications effort more complex?

799. What did the people around you say about it?

800. What new behaviours are required?

801. What is going to be done differently?

3.0 Executing Process Group: Service Application

802. Do schedule issues conflicts?

803. How well did the chosen processes fit the needs of the Service Application project?

804. What is the shortest possible time it will take to complete this Service Application project?

805. Are escalated issues resolved promptly?

806. How can your organization use a weighted decision matrix to evaluate proposals as part of source selection?

807. Who will provide training?

808. What is in place for ensuring adequate change control on Service Application projects that involve outside contracts?

809. How well did the team follow the chosen processes?

810. Will additional funds be needed for hardware or software?

811. What type of people would you want on your team?

812. Could a new application negatively affect the

current IT infrastructure?

813. How do you enter durations, link tasks, and view critical path information?

814. Do the partners have sufficient financial capacity to keep up the benefits produced by the programme?

815. When is the appropriate time to bring the scorecard to Board meetings?

816. Does the Service Application project team have enough people to execute the Service Application project plan?

817. When will the Service Application project be done?

818. What are deliverables of your Service Application project?

819. What areas were overlooked on this Service Application project?

820. How many different communication channels does the Service Application project team have?

3.1 Team Member Status Report: Service Application

821. Does your organization have the means (staff, money, contract, etc.) to produce or to acquire the product, good, or service?

822. When a teams productivity and success depend on collaboration and the efficient flow of information, what generally fails them?

823. Why is it to be done?

824. Are the products of your organizations Service Application projects meeting customers objectives?

825. How will resource planning be done?

826. How it is to be done?

827. Do you have an Enterprise Service Application project Management Office (EPMO)?

828. Does every department have to have a Service Application project Manager on staff?

829. Does the product, good, or service already exist within your organization?

830. Are the attitudes of staff regarding Service Application project work improving?

831. How can you make it practical?

832. What is to be done?

833. Is there evidence that staff is taking a more professional approach toward management of your organizations Service Application projects?

834. Will the staff do training or is that done by a third party?

835. What specific interest groups do you have in place?

836. How does this product, good, or service meet the needs of the Service Application project and your organization as a whole?

837. The problem with Reward & Recognition Programs is that the truly deserving people all too often get left out. How can you make it practical?

838. Are your organizations Service Application projects more successful over time?

839. How much risk is involved?

3.2 Change Request: Service Application

840. How are the measures for carrying out the change established?

841. How many times must the change be modified or presented to the change control board before it is approved?

842. Where do changes come from?

843. How to get changes (code) out in a timely manner?

844. What are the requirements for urgent changes?

845. Should staff call into the helpdesk or go to the website?

846. Will this change conflict with other requirements changes (e.g., lead to conflicting operational scenarios)?

847. How many lines of code must be changed to implement the change?

848. When to submit a change request?

849. Should a more thorough impact analysis be conducted?

850. What is the change request log?

851. Has your address changed?

852. Will there be a change request form in use?

853. Who is responsible to authorize changes?

854. Will new change requests be acknowledged in a timely manner?

855. Who is responsible for the implementation and monitoring of all measures?

856. What is the relationship between requirements attributes and reliability?

857. What are the basic mechanics of the Change Advisory Board (CAB)?

858. How is quality being addressed on the Service Application project?

3.3 Change Log: Service Application

859. When was the request submitted?

860. Is the submitted change a new change or a modification of a previously approved change?

861. How does this change affect scope?

862. Do the described changes impact on the integrity or security of the system?

863. Who initiated the change request?

864. Does the suggested change request represent a desired enhancement to the products functionality?

865. Is the change request open, closed or pending?

866. How does this relate to the standards developed for specific business processes?

867. Is this a mandatory replacement?

868. How does this change affect the timeline of the schedule?

869. Is the requested change request a result of changes in other Service Application project(s)?

870. Does the suggested change request seem to represent a necessary enhancement to the product?

871. Will the Service Application project fail if the

change request is not executed?

872. When was the request approved?

873. Is the change backward compatible without limitations?

874. Is the change request within Service Application project scope?

3.4 Decision Log: Service Application

875. How does the use a Decision Support System influence the strategies/tactics or costs?

876. What is the line where eDiscovery ends and document review begins?

877. With whom was the decision shared or considered?

878. How does provision of information, both in terms of content and presentation, influence acceptance of alternative strategies?

879. What makes you different or better than others companies selling the same thing?

880. Adversarial environment. is your opponent open to a non-traditional workflow, or will it likely challenge anything you do?

881. Meeting purpose; why does this team meet?

882. How does an increasing emphasis on cost containment influence the strategies and tactics used?

883. How consolidated and comprehensive a story can you tell by capturing currently available incident data in a central location and through a log of key decisions during an incident?

884. Does anything need to be adjusted?

885. What eDiscovery problem or issue did your organization set out to fix or make better?

886. How effective is maintaining the log at facilitating organizational learning?

887. What is the average size of your matters in an applicable measurement?

888. What is your overall strategy for quality control / quality assurance procedures?

889. What alternatives/risks were considered?

890. Is your opponent open to a non-traditional workflow, or will it likely challenge anything you do?

891. Who will be given a copy of this document and where will it be kept?

892. How do you define success?

893. Decision-making process; how will the team make decisions?

894. Do strategies and tactics aimed at less than full control reduce the costs of management or simply shift the cost burden?

3.5 Quality Audit: Service Application

895. Are the policies and processes, as set out in the Quality Audit Manual, properly applied?

896. What has changed/improved as a result of the review processes?

897. Will the evidence likely be sufficient and appropriate?

898. How does your organization know that the range and quality of its accommodation, catering and transportation services are appropriately effective and constructive?

899. How does the organization know that its industry and community engagement planning and management systems are appropriately effective and constructive in enabling relationships with key stakeholder groups?

900. How does your organization know that its system for commercializing research outputs is appropriately effective and constructive?

901. Are there appropriate indicators for monitoring the effectiveness and efficiency of processes?

902. How does your organization know that its systems for meeting staff extracurricular learning support requirements are appropriately effective and constructive?

903. How does your organization know that it provides a safe and healthy environment?

904. How does your organization know that the support for its staff is appropriately effective and constructive?

905. Are all records associated with the reconditioning of a device maintained for a minimum of two years after the sale or disposal of the last device within a lot of merchandise?

906. How does your organization know that its advisory services are appropriately effective and constructive?

907. How well do you think your organization engages with the outside community?

908. How does the organization know that its system for maintaining and advancing the capabilities of its staff, particularly in relation to the Mission of the organization, is appropriately effective and constructive?

909. Are goals well supported with strategies, operational plans, manuals and training?

910. What data about organizational performance is routinely collected and reported?

911. What experience do staff have in the type of work that the audit entails?

912. How does your organization know that its system for attending to the health and wellbeing of its staff is

appropriately effective and constructive?

913. How does your organization know that its systems for assisting staff with career planning and employment placements are appropriately effective and constructive?

914. How does your organization know that its risk management system is appropriately effective and constructive?

3.6 Team Directory: Service Application

915. When does information need to be distributed?

916. Who will be the stakeholders on your next Service Application project?

917. Where should the information be distributed?

918. Process decisions: how well was task order work performed?

919. Process decisions: is work progressing on schedule and per contract requirements?

920. Who will report Service Application project status to all stakeholders?

921. Where will the product be used and/or delivered or built when appropriate?

922. What are you going to deliver or accomplish?

923. Process decisions: do job conditions warrant additional actions to collect job information and document on-site activity?

924. Process decisions: are all start-up, turn over and close out requirements of the contract satisfied?

925. Who are your stakeholders (customers, sponsors, end users, team members)?

926. Is construction on schedule?

927. How will you accomplish and manage the objectives?

928. How do unidentified risks impact the outcome of the Service Application project?

929. Process decisions: which organizational elements and which individuals will be assigned management functions?

930. What needs to be communicated?

931. Who are the Team Members?

932. Days from the time the issue is identified?

933. Decisions: is the most suitable form of contract being used?

934. Have you decided when to celebrate the Service Application projects completion date?

3.7 Team Operating Agreement: Service Application

935. Must your members collaborate successfully to complete Service Application projects?

936. Are there more than two native languages represented by your team?

937. What is group supervision?

938. Is compensation based on team and individual performance?

939. Are there more than two functional areas represented by your team?

940. What is culture?

941. Are there differences in access to communication and collaboration technology based on team member location?

942. How will group handle unplanned absences?

943. Do you prevent individuals from dominating the meeting?

944. To whom do you deliver your services?

945. Confidentiality: how will confidential information be handled?

946. Do you listen for voice tone and word choice to understand the meaning behind words?

947. What are the boundaries (organizational or geographic) within which you operate?

948. What administrative supports will be put in place to support the team and the teams supervisor?

949. Do you begin with a question to engage everyone?

950. Do you post any action items, due dates, and responsibilities on the team website?

951. Have you set the goals and objectives of the team?

952. The method to be used in the decision making process; Will it be consensus, majority rule, or the supervisor having the final say?

953. What individual strengths does each team member bring to the group?

954. Are there more than two national cultures represented by your team?

3.8 Team Performance Assessment: Service Application

955. To what degree does the teams approach to its work allow for modification and improvement over time?

956. Social categorization and intergroup behaviour: Does minimal intergroup discrimination make social identity more positive?

957. To what degree do the goals specify concrete team work products?

958. How do you manage human resources?

959. To what degree does the team possess adequate membership to achieve its ends?

960. If you have received criticism from reviewers that your work suffered from method variance, what was the circumstance?

961. To what degree do team members frequently explore the teams purpose and its implications?

962. To what degree can all members engage in open and interactive considerations?

963. What structural changes have you made or are you preparing to make?

964. When a reviewer complains about method

variance, what is the essence of the complaint?

965. To what degree will the team ensure that all members equitably share the work essential to the success of the team?

966. To what degree does the teams purpose constitute a broader, deeper aspiration than just accomplishing short-term goals?

967. Can team performance be reliably measured in simulator and live exercises using the same assessment tool?

968. To what degree can team members vigorously define the teams purpose in considerations with others who are not part of the functioning team?

969. To what degree do team members understand one anothers roles and skills?

970. When does the medium matter?

971. If you have criticized someones work for method variance in your role as reviewer, what was the circumstance?

972. Can familiarity breed backup?

973. To what degree are corresponding categories of skills either actually or potentially represented across the membership?

974. How much interpersonal friction is there in your team?

3.9 Team Member Performance Assessment: Service Application

975. What tools are available to determine whether all contract functional and compliance areas of performance objectives, measures, and incentives have been met?

976. How will they be formed?

977. To what degree do team members feel that the purpose of the team is important, if not exciting?

978. To what degree do team members articulate the teams work approach?

979. What is a significant fact or event?

980. How do you currently use the time that is available?

981. How do you work together to improve teaching and learning?

982. Goals met?

983. In what areas would you like to concentrate your knowledge and resources?

984. How is the timing of assessments organized (e.g., pre/post-test, single point during training, multiple reassessment during training)?

985. What are the standards or expectations for success?

986. Who receives a benchmark visit?

987. To what extent are systems and applications (e.g., game engine, mobile device platform) utilized?

988. To what degree do members articulate the goals beyond the team membership?

989. To what degree are the skill areas critical to team performance present?

990. Are any governance changes sufficient to impact achievement?

991. What is used as a basis for instructional decisions?

992. To what degree is the team cognizant of small wins to be celebrated along the way?

3.10 Issue Log: Service Application

993. What help do you and your team need from the stakeholders?

994. What effort will a change need?

995. What is a change?

996. Who do you turn to if you have questions?

997. Do you feel a register helps?

998. Who is the issue assigned to?

999. How do you reply to this question; you am new here and managing this major program. How do you suggest you build your network?

1000. Are there common objectives between the team and the stakeholder?

1001. Do you feel more overwhelmed by stakeholders?

1002. Is the issue log kept in a safe place?

1003. How is this initiative related to other portfolios, programs, or Service Application projects?

1004. Is access to the Issue Log controlled?

1005. What are the typical contents?

4.0 Monitoring and Controlling Process Group: Service Application

1006. What factors are contributing to progress or delay in the achievement of products and results?

1007. Specific - is the objective clear in terms of what, how, when, and where the situation will be changed?

1008. Based on your Service Application project communication management plan, what worked well?

1009. How well defined and documented were the Service Application project management processes you chose to use?

1010. Is progress on outcomes due to your program?

1011. How is agile portfolio management done?

1012. Are the services being delivered?

1013. How were collaborations developed, and how are they sustained?

1014. What input will you be required to provide the Service Application project team?

1015. Did the Service Application project team have enough people to execute the Service Application project plan?

1016. Is the program in place as intended?

1017. Is it what was agreed upon?

1018. Were sponsors and decision makers available when needed outside regularly scheduled meetings?

1019. Change, where should you look for problems?

1020. How should needs be met?

1021. User: who wants the information and what are they interested in?

1022. Just how important is your work to the overall success of the Service Application project?

4.1 Project Performance Report: Service Application

1023. To what degree does the funding match the requirement?

1024. To what degree will each member have the opportunity to advance his or her professional skills in all three of the above categories while contributing to the accomplishment of the teams purpose and goals?

1025. To what degree are the demands of the task compatible with and converge with the relationships of the informal organization?

1026. To what degree is there a sense that only the team can succeed?

1027. Next Steps?

1028. To what degree are the teams goals and objectives clear, simple, and measurable?

1029. To what degree do the relationships of the informal organization motivate taskrelevant behavior and facilitate task completion?

1030. To what degree are the members clear on what they are individually responsible for and what they are jointly responsible for?

1031. To what degree does the teams work approach provide opportunity for members to engage in fact-based problem solving?

1032. To what degree do individual skills and abilities match task demands?

1033. To what degree are fresh input and perspectives systematically caught and added (for example, through information and analysis, new members, and senior sponsors)?

1034. What is the degree to which rules govern information exchange between groups?

1035. To what degree do all members feel responsible for all agreed-upon measures?

1036. To what degree does the informal organization make use of individual resources and meet individual needs?

1037. To what degree does the information network communicate information relevant to the task?

1038. What is in it for you?

4.2 Variance Analysis: Service Application

1039. What should management do?

1040. Can process improvements lead to unfavorable variances?

1041. How does your organization measure performance?

1042. Are estimates of costs at completion generated in a rational, consistent manner?

1043. How does the use of a single conversion element (rather than the traditional labor and overhead elements) affect standard costing?

1044. Do you identify potential or actual budget-based and time-based schedule variances?

1045. What types of services and expense are shared between business segments?

1046. How are material, labor, and overhead standards set?

1047. How do you evaluate the impact of schedule changes, work around, et?

1048. Other relevant issues of Variance Analysis -selling price or gross margin?

1049. How do you identify and isolate causes of favorable and unfavorable cost and schedule variances?

1050. There are detailed schedules which support control account and work package start and completion dates/events?

1051. What are the direct labor dollars and/or hours?

1052. Do the rates and prices remain constant throughout the year?

1053. Are the wbs and organizational levels for application of the Service Application projected overhead costs identified?

1054. Does the contractors system provide unit or lot costs when applicable?

1055. Who are responsible for overhead performance control of related costs?

1056. Are meaningful indicators identified for use in measuring the status of cost and schedule performance?

1057. Are significant decision points, constraints, and interfaces identified as key milestones?

4.3 Earned Value Status: Service Application

1058. How does this compare with other Service Application projects?

1059. What is the unit of forecast value?

1060. When is it going to finish?

1061. Where are your problem areas?

1062. Validation is a process of ensuring that the developed system will actually achieve the stakeholders desired outcomes; Are you building the right product? What do you validate?

1063. Are you hitting your Service Application projects targets?

1064. Earned value can be used in almost any Service Application project situation and in almost any Service Application project environment. it may be used on large Service Application projects, medium sized Service Application projects, tiny Service Application projects (in cut-down form), complex and simple Service Application projects and in any market sector. some people, of course, know all about earned value, they have used it for years - but perhaps not as effectively as they could have?

1065. Where is evidence-based earned value in your organization reported?

1066. If earned value management (EVM) is so good in determining the true status of a Service Application project and Service Application project its completion, why is it that hardly any one uses it in information systems related Service Application projects?

1067. How much is it going to cost by the finish?

1068. Verification is a process of ensuring that the developed system satisfies the stakeholders agreements and specifications; Are you building the product right? What do you verify?

4.4 Risk Audit: Service Application

1069. Do staff understand the extent of duty of care?

1070. Have customers been involved fully in the definition of requirements?

1071. When your organization is entering into a major contract, does it seek legal advice?

1072. Whence the business risk audit?

1073. Does the Service Application project team have experience with the technology to be implemented?

1074. Should additional substantive testing be conducted because of the risk audit results?

1075. Is the number of people on the Service Application project team adequate to do the job?

1076. How do you compare to other jurisdictions when managing the risk of ....?

1077. Are procedures in place to ensure the security of staff and information and compliance with privacy legislation if applicable?

1078. Have all involved been advised of any obligations they have to sponsors?

1079. Are you willing to seek legal advice when required?

1080. Are duties out-of-class?

1081. Is there (or should there be) some impact on the process of setting materiality when the auditor more effectively identifies higher risk areas of the financial statements?

1082. Does your organization have any policies or procedures to guide its decision-making (code of conduct for the board, conflict of interest policy, etc.)?

1083. To what extent are auditors effective at linking business risks and management assertions?

1084. Do you have a clear plan for the future that describes what you want to do and how you are going to do it?

1085. What are the legal implications of not identifying a complete universe of business risks?

1086. Do you meet all obligations relating to funds secured from grants, loans and sponsors?

1087. How risk averse are you?

4.5 Contractor Status Report: Service Application

1088. What was the final actual cost?

1089. Are there contractual transfer concerns?

1090. What was the budget or estimated cost for your organizations services?

1091. If applicable; describe your standard schedule for new software version releases. Are new software version releases included in the standard maintenance plan?

1092. Who can list a Service Application project as organization experience, your organization or a previous employee of your organization?

1093. How does the proposed individual meet each requirement?

1094. How long have you been using the services?

1095. What are the minimum and optimal bandwidth requirements for the proposed solution?

1096. Describe how often regular updates are made to the proposed solution. Are corresponding regular updates included in the standard maintenance plan?

1097. What is the average response time for answering a support call?

1098. What process manages the contracts?

1099. What was the overall budget or estimated cost?

1100. How is risk transferred?

1101. What was the actual budget or estimated cost for your organizations services?

4.6 Formal Acceptance: Service Application

1102. How does your team plan to obtain formal acceptance on your Service Application project?

1103. What was done right?

1104. What features, practices, and processes proved to be strengths or weaknesses?

1105. Was the sponsor/customer satisfied?

1106. Was the client satisfied with the Service Application project results?

1107. Does it do what Service Application project team said it would?

1108. General estimate of the costs and times to complete the Service Application project?

1109. Is formal acceptance of the Service Application project product documented and distributed?

1110. Do you buy-in installation services?

1111. Was the Service Application project work done on time, within budget, and according to specification?

1112. Who supplies data?

1113. Do you perform formal acceptance or burn-in tests?

1114. Who would use it?

1115. What lessons were learned about your Service Application project management methodology?

1116. Was the Service Application project goal achieved?

1117. Was the Service Application project managed well?

1118. What is the Acceptance Management Process?

1119. Did the Service Application project achieve its MOV?

1120. Was business value realized?

1121. What function(s) does it fill or meet?

5.0 Closing Process Group: Service Application

1122. What is the overall risk of the Service Application project to your organization?

1123. Is this a follow-on to a previous Service Application project?

1124. What is the risk of failure to your organization?

1125. What was learned?

1126. Is there a clear cause and effect between the activity and the lesson learned?

1127. Is this a follow-on to a previous Service Application project?

1128. What areas does the group agree are the biggest success on the Service Application project?

1129. Did you do things well?

1130. Is this an updated Service Application project Proposal Document?

1131. Did the Service Application project management methodology work?

1132. Contingency planning. if a risk event occurs, what will you do?

1133. How well did you do?

1134. What level of risk does the proposed budget represent to the Service Application project?

1135. What is an Encumbrance?

1136. What is the Service Application project Management Process?

5.1 Procurement Audit: Service Application

1137. Are all purchase orders cancelled after payment to avoid duplicate payment of the same invoice?

1138. Are budget transfers within the general fund made for only the already stated items permitted by law and regulation?

1139. Are lease-purchase agreements drawn and processed in accordance with law and regulation?

1140. Are there policies regarding special approval for capital expenditures?

1141. Does the procurement Service Application project comply with European Communities regulations and rules?

1142. Are there reasonable procedures to identify possible sources of supply?

1143. Is there an approval policy in which the final cost of an order exceeds the amount originally estimated on the requisition or purchase order?

1144. Has it been determined which areas of procurement the audit should cover?

1145. Were exclusion causes duly considered before the actual evaluation of tenders?

1146. Do the internal control systems function appropriate?

1147. Did your organization decide for an appropriate and admissible procurement procedure?

1148. Is there any objection?

1149. Is free and fair (international) competition promoted by organizational policies and legislation, in line with legal, trade organizations and other policies?

1150. Is the departments procurement function/unit well organized?

1151. Is there no evidence of collusion between bidders?

1152. Does the cash disbursement policy prohibit drawing checks to cash or bearer?

1153. Are the purchase order forms designed for efficient and simple completion?

1154. Are transportation charges verified?

1155. Are the established budget and timetable (milestones) respected?

1156. Has management taken the necessary steps to ensure that relevant control systems are always up to date?

5.2 Contract Close-Out: Service Application

1157. Was the contract complete without requiring numerous changes and revisions?

1158. Was the contract sufficiently clear so as not to result in numerous disputes and misunderstandings?

1159. Parties: who is involved?

1160. Have all contracts been completed?

1161. Are the signers the authorized officials?

1162. How/when used ?

1163. Was the contract type appropriate?

1164. Have all contract records been included in the Service Application project archives?

1165. Change in knowledge?

1166. What is capture management?

1167. Change in circumstances?

1168. Have all acceptance criteria been met prior to final payment to contractors?

1169. Parties: Authorized?

1170. How does it work?

1171. Have all contracts been closed?

1172. Change in attitude or behavior?

1173. Has each contract been audited to verify acceptance and delivery?

1174. What happens to the recipient of services?

1175. How is the contracting office notified of the automatic contract close-out?

5.3 Project or Phase Close-Out: Service Application

1176. What benefits or impacts does the stakeholder group expect to obtain as a result of the Service Application project?

1177. Is the lesson significant, valid, and applicable?

1178. Who controlled the resources for the Service Application project?

1179. What is this stakeholder expecting?

1180. If you were the Service Application project sponsor, how would you determine which Service Application project team(s) and/or individuals deserve recognition?

1181. Were cost budgets met?

1182. Were risks identified and mitigated?

1183. What are the informational communication needs for each stakeholder?

1184. Complete yes or no?

1185. What is the information level of detail required for each stakeholder?

1186. In preparing the Lessons Learned report, should it reflect a consensus viewpoint, or should the report reflect the different individual viewpoints?

1187. What advantages do the an individual interview have over a group meeting, and vice-versa?

1188. Was the user/client satisfied with the end product?

1189. Have business partners been involved extensively, and what data was required for them?

1190. What security considerations needed to be addressed during the procurement life cycle?

1191. What is a Risk?

1192. How often did each stakeholder need an update?

1193. What could be done to improve the process?

1194. Who are the Service Application project stakeholders and what are roles and involvement?

5.4 Lessons Learned: Service Application

1195. What is the supplier dependency?

1196. What did you do right?

1197. To what extent was the evolution of risks communicated?

1198. What is in the future?

1199. Why do you need to measure?

1200. Are you in full regulatory compliance?

1201. How well does the product or service the Service Application project produced meet your needs?

1202. What is your organizations performance history?

1203. What is the quality and content of communication?

1204. Which estimation issues did you personally have and what was the impact?

1205. What things surprised you on the Service Application project that were not in the plan?

1206. What regulatory regime controlled how your

organization head and program manager directed your organization and Service Application project?

1207. What on the Service Application project worked well and was effective in the delivery of the product?

1208. How effectively were issues resolved before escalation was necessary?

1209. How much of your time was spent on other than this Service Application project?

1210. How often did you violate the rules?

1211. How many government and contractor personnel are authorized for the Service Application project?

1212. How much flexibility is there in the funding (e.g., what authorities does the program manager have to change to the specifics of the funding within the overall funding ceiling)?

1213. What worked well/did not work well?

Index

263

dictates   169
Dictionary   3, 148
difference   123, 162
different   7, 19, 35, 37, 40, 42, 72, 111, 129, 131, 179, 189,
197, 208, 211, 218, 253
difficult 72, 153, 158, 162, 165, 173, 176
dilemma   110
dimensions   20
direct   237
directed   255
direction   31, 58
directly 1, 62, 69, 148
Directory   5, 223
Disagree   12, 17, 29, 45, 59, 75, 90, 102
disaster   54-55, 168
disclosed   205
disclosure   99
discussion   114
displayed   35, 60, 152
disposal   221
disputes   250
disqualify   71
disruptive   66
Divided   27, 31, 44, 58, 74, 89, 101, 121
document   11, 43, 123, 132, 138, 144-145, 202, 218-219, 223,
246
documented 42, 80, 84, 90, 93, 96, 100, 142, 144, 178, 186-187,
207, 232, 244
documents   7, 142
dollars 237
domains   84
dominating   225
dormant   110
drawing   249
Driver   62
drivers 58, 62
drives   57
driving 102, 120
duplicate   248
Duration   4, 147, 159, 164, 166
durations   37, 151, 169, 211
during 31, 88, 124, 145, 160, 185, 198, 200, 203, 218, 229, 253
duties   241